Once Again

Dr Om Prakash Yadava

DEDICATION

This book is dedicated to the people of North-East of India particularly to HB Jaichand Singh who was author's classmate in M. Sc at the University of Allahabad during 1964-65.

-    Dr Om Prakash Yadava

Contents

ACKNOWLEDGMENTS

Author is highly indebted to the inspiration which he received from his surroundings, wife and daughter to peep into the human relations in light of disturbances of 1971 which led to formation of Bangladesh.

PROLOGUE

"Can you meet me once?"

"No, I don't want to."

"In case you don't like to come to my place, I am ready to come to your place or if you feel like, we may meet at some other place."

"Why unnecessarily you are asking me for something which is not practicable and also has no relevance."

"Why are you making yourself so hard, you had never been a man like that."

"See things have changed with the time, neither you are the same Malini, nor I am same Mridul. Last over forty years we never knew, who was where and who was in what shape?"

"That is something which was not in our hands. Despite all our best efforts we became the victims of circumstances and therefore let us forget the past."

"You are making the things so simple but it is not that simple to forget what has been missed and what changed the entire course of my life."

"I can understand your agony and anguish but something was probably destined and that happened."

"Then where is the problem, whatever is happening is also destined and let it happen."

"You are right but destiny never asks us not to make efforts or not to try to choose a better path."

"Though you may be right but now your voice is not going to attract me and better we leave where the things are."

"OK, I know you feel hurt. Alright think it over with a cool mind, I will give a ring after a couple of days."

Discussion over telephone discontinued; Mridul placed receiver on the cradle and went away to his study room. He had developed a practice that whenever he felt disturbed, he would go to his study- room, take out some book from the shelf and go on turning over the pages; sometimes standing near the shelf and sometimes he would sit in the chair placed near the table which could be called the study table. Unmindfully he took out a thick book and started turning over the pages standing by the side of the table that suddenly his eyes fell on a page having text in Sanskrit with narration in English and only then he could realize that the book in his hand was nothing but Srimad Bhagwat Geeta and the text & its narration on that page were reading as,

"I am the inflamed Kala(time)the destroyer of the worlds. My purpose here is to destroy these people. Even without you all these warriors arrayed in the enemy's camp will not survive. Therefore, you arise and win the glory; conquering foes, enjoy the affluent Kingdom. These warriors stand already slain by me; be you only an instrument, Arjuna."

The words of Lord Krishna as spoken to Arjuna in the midst of the armies ready for the war which had produced magical effects diverted the line of thought of Mridul and a lot of anger that he had for Malini slowly started melting down. He thought probably the train of events that he had in his life was preordained and were beyond his control but even still he was not able to reconcile with the behavior of Malini before her marriage and which had penetrated deep in his psyche.

"At least she could have sent a message conveying me that she had been forced in

a matrimonial alliance against her wishes and could have asked me to forget her. She had enough time and resources for that through our common friend Saroj who was known to be always in touch with her but she did not do that and left me in a lurch."

This was the thought which remained piercing him and he was not able to comfort himself and was also not in a mood to forgive Malini though he had landed in a state of conflict within his own mind. But that thought had overpowered him to such an extent that he was not able to consider what compulsions might have been there before Malini to succumb to the circumstances and disappear into darkness away from him. The mental churning continued and the thoughts and feelings emanating ultimately mellowed him down to accept her proposal of meeting somewhere just to see what for she wanted to meet him.

"Mridul, may I remind you of my request."
Spoke Malini on the phone after a couple
of days.

Though not very happy to receive the telephone call yet Mridul restrained himself and simply replied,

"I very well remember your request but let me have some more time to consider whether we should meet."

A couple of days passed by and Mridul remained engrossed in mental churning whether to meet Malini or not. His memories and experiences of past which had given him many years of agony were prompting him not to go on the path which he had already abandoned but the lines of Geeta that time was the supreme, were advising him to forget the past and see what she had to say and what for she wanted to meet him. Ultimately good senses prevailed to him and he decided to meet her and listen to her, however, with a totally dispassionate sense having no attachment with whatsoever of the past.

One evening, willy-nilly, he rang her and wanted to see her response,

"Hello, I am Malini, who is on the other end?"

"Mridul; I have considered your request and am ready to meet you at any place except our residences but it will not be for more than half an hour. Place and time, you decide and let me know, however, before coming Sunday."

"Ok"

But something happened and Malini could not keep the enthusiasm & ebullience that she had for meeting with him. However, as she had taken the first step, it was not good to retrace back and she decided to have a meeting on next Saturday evening in the nearby park and informed him of the same.

They met on the specified day at the pre-decided place and exchanged courtesies. Both were wonderstruck to see each other. Malini - the most beautiful girl of the college and most sought after for every extra-curricular activity was looking sinking and fragile with whitish hairs & with tinge of wrinkles on the face and Mridul, a handsome boy full of life, energy and intelligence looked as an aged person with bald head, bespectacled and sunken cheeks. In fact, both of them got shocked to see each other and felt not to have met with. Beauty, vigour and liveliness of each other which was in their mind would not have got shattered like that.

"Why have you decided to leave the worldly life and join the monastery and the social service Organization?" Asked Malini *without any formality.*

"Nothing more is left for me. My son is settled abroad and here I am all alone. He asks me to sell out all property & live with

him but I don't like that. It would be better that remaining days of my life are gainfully utilized and also that I would get company of other similar people."

"But you were very good in dramatics and writing plays etc, why don't you utilize that for arousing social reforms and good to the society."

"That is something which needs element of life and that I have already lost."

"It is something which we decide and act upon. If you accept to-day as it is and utilize it in the gainful manner, life does not end."

"Though I tend to agree with you but somehow I am not getting any urge from inside to remain in active worldly life and also I am all alone."

"Then why don't you go to your son and be with grand-children."

"I have gone there earlier and did not like the things. My son and daughter-in-law both remain busy in their work and children have their own world. I become totally alone and misfit; and outside the house everything is unknown to me and nobody appears with whom I can talk for a little while. At least here I am not a foreigner."

"So your decision to relinquish the worldly life is final."

"As it stands to-day."

"But is not that running away from life?"

"Let that be so."

They remained there for sometimes talking formally about their children, their problems and perspectives and the life and how it was passing just like two acquaintances who had met after a long time but none of them touched any aspect of their past life and also they did not touch upon anything regarding their future life.

Having a very cold & charmless meeting for about fifteen minutes they bade good bye to each other and parted away to their residences leaving behind a trail of hollowness and vacuum to each other. Mridul felt repentant to have met her and possibly Malini also had the same feeling.

Mridul had virtually lost whatsoever residual memories of the good past were there in the finest corners of his mind and he thought that night,

Time is the biggest teacher and to-day again it has given me a lesson.

CHAPTER - I

<u>Repentance</u>

$\mathcal{M}$alini was repenting on her behavior shown towards Mridul. It was on her repeated instance that he had agreed to meet her and when the meeting took place she had dragged her feet and the whole episode ended in a cold swing.

"I still don't understand what went wrong to me that the person whom I had loved, I had adorned and whom I have had been remembering for so many years, suddenly I became so formal and behaved so indifferently. I regret to myself and my behavior and also what he would be feeling about me. Possibly if any negative feeling he has for me would also envelope him."

Was the train of thoughts going on in her mind but she was not really able to identify that how could she behave so indifferent as she had never behaved like that with anybody. Then she remembered the unwelcome happenings on that day when she received an unwelcome telephone call from a colleague whom she never liked because of his dirty habits and who shamelessly had been proposing to marry her which had probably disturbed her and might be due to its effect she could not maintain herself composed & comfortable in her usual manner. Various thoughts were coming to her mind and disappearing away and she could not know that the last ray of Sun had vaned away in the western horizon. She was so much so engrossed in her thoughts that she had virtually forgotten her surroundings; suddenly the door-bell rang and her attention got diverted. She rushed to the door to see who was there and who had rung the bell. As she opened the door she had a pleasant surprise to see her only son standing at the door who hurriedly touched her feet and entered the house with a bag in his hands and she followed him.

"I am very happy my son that you have come to me but why did you not give me any indication that you were coming, I would have prepared your favorite eatables and kept them ready."

"Don't worry Mummy, whatever you make is tasty for me. I had come on duty to the nearby city and was to go back after completing the job but fortunately my work got completed early so I thought of seeing you and then return back."

"Oh! Good. Very good. I am very glad to see you here. Your presence will delight me and also my solitude will go away as long as you are here."

"Yes Mummy. But you know, I have been missing you for very long and this time our telephonic contact has also been much

less. Your grand-daughter Mini also misses you very much. Why don't you come and stay with us?"

"May be you are right. Being alone is a very difficult job but possibly that is my destiny. I do not want to part away this house which is full of memories of my struggles and your childhood days and wandering in those memories I pass my time."

"I also don't want this house to be sold away but you can live either with me or with my elder step brother who no more dislikes you or sometimes with him and sometimes with me."

I have heard enough of you, my son! Now relax and wash yourself. I prepare some tea and snacks for you, first have that and if you like you can see your friend Suresh who has been asking me about you and in the meantime I will prepare dinner. Whatever you like to discuss, we can do that during dinner.

Nilesh went with his bag to his room. After twenty minutes he came back refreshed to his mother and asked for tea which was ready by then. They both sat side by side in the sofa and started sipping tea with occasional munching of savories.

"My son! how is my grand-daughter and what is she doing now?"

"Mini is ok. She is very smart but very naughty and always does whatever she likes but misses you very much and often asks when will Dadi (grand-mother) come?"

"I also badly miss her and during night hours when I am all alone, feel extremely bad but probably God! wants me to be like that."

"Why don't you come and be with us?"

"See, your flat is very small and with my being there you all land in problem and then during day time when you both are out I become totally alone having no body around even to speak a word. On Sunday and other off days, you are having your own engagement where mostly I become misfit. Here at least I have got many people known to me and there are several students who come to me for guidance and coaching which keeps me engaged."

"I understand your problem but in such a lonely house you live alone and also have to cook for yourself and moreover your safety is another great concern."

"That is right but all my neighbours know me and they look after my safety & security and above all God is there to take care of me. As long as I can manage, things are alright and when I become totally helpless I would like to move to an old age home. I don't like to be a burden on my children."

"I don't know, why do you feel yourself to be a burden but any way only I request you to rethink and still you have enough time."

He finished the tea and took mother's nod to go to his friend's house asking her to prepare something very light as he may have to take something with his friend. House of Suresh was at a walkable distance and he decided to walk down to that place.

Malini got herself busy in preparing dinner for herself and her son. It was long after that she was cooking full meals in the evening because being alone she was making enough of meals during day time which was serving her lunch and dinner both. Only thing that she did was that she may make sometimes readymade soup and warm the food for taking during dinner. Though she liked to cook items of her son's choice but she knew that he would definitely take something with his friend and therefore she concentrated only on making simple curry, rice and bread.

Nilesh came back very late in the night as he had met his friend after a very long time and they remained busy in chit chatting with each other and Suresh's wife had insisted him to take dinner with them. Though he told that mother would be cooking something yet he could not resist their demand and took dinner with them. He came back full and was not able to take something at home but feeling for mother he sat with mother and requested her to take dinner which she did very reluctantly.

Next morning, she got up very early as usual, finished her morning routine and sat for Puja which continued till eight hours. By then Nilesh had got up, prepared morning tea in the kitchen and was sipping the same. As he saw his mother having finished her rituals he called her to tea and himself prepared tea for her. While sipping tea she just enquired,

"What is your plan for to-day?"

"You prepare breakfast for me after which I will go to the office of Suresh wherefrom I

will fax progress of my work done to my boss and also make some contacts with my customers. I will come back by lunch hour, may be a little late; take lunch with you and in the evening I plan to return back by the direct train to my place. I have also requested Suresh to arrange a Tatkal ticket for my journey. Will that be alright?"

"It is as per your convenience. I am happy that you are coming back for lunch with me. I only liked that you stayed one day more but any way it is ok."

She enquired in details about the activities of her grand-daughter Mini which Nilesh explained with enthusiasm and thereafter they went ahead to further activities of their respective preparedness.

She went to kitchen to prepare breakfast. Though her son had a taste for non-vegetarian preparations; but she was strictly vegetarian and never allowed anything else to be prepared in her kitchen and that was also one of the reasons why she did not like to live with her son. Around nine thirty hours Nilesh came ready and asked for the breakfast. She gave him the simple breakfast consisting of wheat porridge, some pieces of loaves and milk. He took it and liked mother to prepare vegetables of his liking and went out asking her to close the door.

Nilesh came back at two thirty hours in the afternoon. The lunch had been cooked and was getting cold. He washed himself and came to the dining table. She warmed the food and one by one placed all the items at the dining table. They both sat for taking the meals. A special preparation of cauliflower blended with butter was the most favorite item of Nilesh which only she was able to make and that was specially prepared by her for the son. He enjoyed different items and finished the lunch with a high sense of satisfaction.

"Are you really going back to-day?" Asked the mother.

"Yes, Mum. I have to go back. This is my unplanned visit to you. I will try to come again next month."

"Why don't you bring Neeru sometimes with you. Let her be with me for some days."

"You know, we both are having two different domain of jobs, I am a factory officer and she is a teacher. Our leave and holidays are totally different and they never match. During summers when she had holidays I tried to take leave and come here but due to some urgent orders I did not get leave. I will try to come with her and Mini during coming Dipawali. Will it be ok?"

"For me you all are always welcome, as you feel convenient."

Nilesh went back to his room, packed up his bag and by four hours in the afternoon came to mother ready to move. Malini liked to accompany him up to railway station but he very respectfully asked her not to be troubled as Suresh will reach there to see him off. She came up to the main gate, he touched her feet, hired an auto-rickshaw and moved away. She remained standing there with her eyes filled with tears. Suddenly she remembered the days when Nilesh was a toddler and had started going to Nursery school. He was very timid and always liked to hide himself behind the free end of her Saree and would insist mother to follow him up to school and then come back to pick him up but that was not practicable as she herself had to get ready to go to her school for teaching but, whenever his rickshaw was not coming she used to take him to school on her scooter.

"How shy & timid he was, always taking refuge behind my Saree and would depend on me for every small thing or big thing and now he has no time for that mother."

She thought for a while but next moment she remembered that it was not he but it was time. Now he was not a child but father a child and she had also become a grand-mother.

As that thought vanished the other thought flashed,
"Am I same Malini who was known as the beauty queen of the college and after whom so many students and young teachers were mad?"

And further she thought, "my past is a dream-thought now and whosoever sees me, can't believe that I was a beauty queen. See how things have changed having left behind only memories either to be happy or morose. We may relive in those times only in thoughts & never get them back. We may be able to purchase anything of choice but no body & no amount of money could ever purchase the times gone away."

While she was sinking and floating in the sea of uncontrolled spontaneous train of thoughts, another thought flashed, *"had I resisted and put my foot down against the marriage arranged hurriedly by my father which I could not do then and had I forced for marriage with Mridul, I would not have been alone as I am to-day and possibly what I am to-day and the way Mridul has become indifferent would not have happened."*

She came inside the house and despite her knowledge of Srimad Bhagwat Geeta and its teachings, she could not contain herself and continued with her wayward thoughts. Though enough food was available for dinner but she did not feel like taking anything and went to her bed-room for reading her favorite book to divert her flow of thoughts and thereafter inviting slumber to come and grip her, however, she did realize that,

"it was not possible to get out of the past & its effects and those memories either delight or torment till we say good bye to the world though while those events were

happening such a thing would have never been realized, anticipated, appreciated or even imagined."

Anything that happens leaves an indelible imprint on the canvas of time.

.

CHAPTER – II

Wings of Heart

$\mathcal{S}$he remembered that she was the second and last child of her parents. Her elder brother was eight years senior to her and was a very brilliant student having a longing for doing something extraordinary in his life. She had no remembrance of her very early child hood but she had faint memories of those days when she had started going to first standard. The head mistress of the school was very close to her father who had been a senior inspector of schools of her state and all teachers used to take enough care of her. In the school she always wore prescribed dress but outside she was attired nicely by her mother to look like a fairy and people used to call her as butterfly. As she grew up, she also came out a brilliant student and a lovely girl, her mother being extremely careful about her daily routine, friends, what all she did in the school, home work and of course get up and manners. She continued in the same school up to matriculation under an environment of care and protection. Though she had inclination towards extra-curricular activities and badminton but they were encouraged in the school and its programs only.

Her father was strict disciplinarian and conservative and maintained decorum in every activity of life. Get up at five in the morning, finish off your daily routine, take bath and sit for Puja at least for fifteen minutes and then complete home work if something left over in the night, take breakfast and proceed to school. Similarly, in the evening after returning back from school; take tiffin, relax for half an hour, if like play some games in the house premises along with known children of neighborhood, then come inside the house & read some religious books for half an hour, take dinner, do your home-work and go to bed positively at ten hours' night. She had followed the routine stereotyped life up to matriculation as long as she was in that School living with her parents.

She had passed matriculation in flying colors and liked to continue her studies in science stream for which she had to move to the nearby city where she was admitted in the most prestigious college. Her accommodation was arranged in the college hostel itself in a double bedded room. Her father and mother both had accompanied her to the city and they ensured her having got properly settled before leaving back for their residence. She found college life totally different from her life hitherto; starting from accommodating with room-mate, hostel food provided in the mess, college hours and teaching curriculum, evenings in the hostel and late hour sleeping after finishing the work assigned in the class and a strange feeling on Sundays and other holidays of one or two days. During long vacations she was coming back home to be with parents but such occasions had become limited.

While she joined college her elder brother had already completed his studies and had joined a multinational Organization. Her father himself came to her to give her monthly expenses for the first six months after which he used to remit her money by money order. Sometimes her elder brother would also remit her some money which she utilized for purchasing clothing and other items of her choice. Her room-mate was an extrovert girl always busy in many side activities while she was more interested in her studies. She experienced a lot of difficulties in adjusting herself with the new city, new environment and the new college with co-education where boys and girls both were studying together and that too particularly at an age when physical &

emotional transformations were taking place by leaps & bounds and also when the care and discipline of parents were missing. The whole environment had offered more of freedom than responsibility coupled with the company of a room-mate who was extrovert, free and hailing from a very open family and whose interest was not studies but everything else.

Though Malini could not contain herself being affected by the changed environment yet the discipline which had been a part of her life always stopped her at a limit and beyond that she never compromised. First year was practically a time span of learning and adjusting with the new environment but her room-mate was successful in teaching her a lesson that studies were not the only thing in life rather there were certain demands of the age & time which called for taking interest in boys also. By the end of the year she sometimes noticed that a fair, handsome boy who was good in studies also was having a keen look at her but she took it very casually as many boys were there who were found discussing about girls and looking at them.

Second year came and each one had become reasonably familiar with each other. Some boys were really very good who were ready to help each other but some were naughty getting pleasure by putting somebody in trouble and difficulties. The Boy who was showing interest in her was Mridul, who had come from some other city and was living in boys' hostel. He was very good in playing badminton also and was participating in the college team and other tournaments. Gradually she also started getting attracted towards him but only in thoughts and there was no other visible sign. One night her room-mate just commented,

"I find you are taking interest in Mridul."

"No, no, there is nothing like that."

"Better you don't like him. Don't become my competitor."

"So you take him away, who stops."

That girl burst into laughter,

"Why are you so serious? I simply wanted to have a fun of you and see whether you also like someone. I don't like him, he is a PARHAKOO (one who is devoted in studies) and such a boy can't cope up with me. I want somebody who is rich and fun loving."

Though that was a fun but that stirred her mind that there was something and possibly others were also noticing something brewing between them. One day while all students were busy in chemistry practical laboratory and the teacher after having explained them the day's work had gone to Principal's office, suddenly there was a loud scream, a painful scream. All students started looking toward the source of sound but Mridul could recognize her voice and immediately ran to her. A little amount of concentrated sulphuric acid had fallen on her hand and due to immense burning she was in pains. He immediately caught hold of her hand, put that under the running water tap and ran to refrigerator and brought some ice cubes which he applied at the place of burn but still she was feeling too much of pains. He continued with the pouring of water and applying ice cubes and as the pain subsided he asked her to come to the college dispensary located at a little distance. The doctor on duty examined her, applied some ointment and bandaged and gave necessary precautionary instructions.

Teacher had received the news and had come back to the laboratory and after a few minutes, Malini came back with Mridul and explained to the teacher of all that had happened. Teacher asked her to go back to the hostel and rest as after a few hours she would be alright. He asked Mridul to escort her up to hostel main gate and come back.

Anyway teacher could understand what would have happened causing such an accident and he specifically advised all the students,

"be extremely careful while handling concentrated sulphuric acid and remember NEVER to add water to concentrated sulphuric acid and also to avoid adding any other liquid to that acid. In case concentrated sulphuric acid was to be diluted, add that acid slowly and carefully through the sides to the water kept in a beaker or some other glass vessel."

Next morning when she came to the class, she specifically went to the seat of Mridul and thanked him profusely for all the help. That small instance became harbinger of a turning point in their relations.

The relation which had germinated out of small instance became more and more melodious as the time passed by, however, none of them expressed anything to each other. As the exams were approaching, classes became much less and everybody concentrated on his/her studies. Months of February and early March saw all the practical examinations in different subjects and from the third week of March the written exams commenced for which exam centers were in different colleges of the city and as a result no one was able to know how the other one was performing?

At the end of exams all students were in a hurry to go back to their parents, however, before leaving they were meeting their teachers and each other for saying good bye because nobody knew how many would be studying together again. One day while Malini was coming out of the chemistry laboratory after saying good bye to her chemistry teacher, she saw Mridul coming to her. She felt very happy but concealing cleverly her expressions, she asked Mridul as he approached her,

"What makes you come here, Teacher told me that you have already met him?"

"I have come here for you."

"Why?"

"I want to know, what is your plan for the next year?"

"I like to study medicine and will try for admission to some medical college through the entrance examination. In case I don't succeed or something goes wrong, I will take admission in B.Sc. in the university proper."

"But what about you?"

"My aim is to compete for civil services and for that it is essential to join humanities stream in the university but my final decision depends on you. If you go to medical stream, I will go to humanities but

if you join B.Sc. I will also join that. Let me see what lies there in the womb of future."
"My God! But why so?"

"I can't follow you in medicine but for graduation I will accompany you. Next year I will apply for admission in humanities as well as in science stream and depending on your admission the final decision will be taken."

"But would you tell me, why do you want to accompany me? We are having our own lives and their separate path"

"You ask your own heart; would it not like me to be with you?"

"Ok. I will ask, whenever, I am free but why can't you tell me?"

"Your heart itself will tell you, what I like to tell you."

She smiled at him and without telling something more liked to go away. They shook hands with each other, wished each other for the best results in the exams and also that their cherished desires to be fulfilled. Heart to heart she felt delighted to know that Mridul cared for her but that was something that was beyond her expression but Mridul could read it.

The language of heart is understood only by a reciprocating heart.

CHAPTER – III

Past Continues

*M*ridul was very keen in the works of Carl Linnaeus and his epoch making formulation of modern taxonomy and paleobotany and he was keeping himself busy in searching for newer varieties of plants hitherto unknown and plant fossils to ascertain evolution of different species. He had requested his posting in the North-East as an officer of botanical survey of India with a view to keep himself too far away from the place where his memories were lying and which had tormented him for many days & nights and still had not gone out of his mind.

He was keeping himself so busy that he got no time to think of anything other than his work.

When his posting orders came his mother was vexed at the news and asked him to make efforts to get that changed as she had no liking for such a far off place; but seeing the interest of Mridul she reluctantly agreed and with a lot of resentment accompanied him to take care of him. He knew the plight of his mother that she would find very tough to adjust herself at a place in an environment which was not at all conducive to her way of living and where the local language was also not known to her. But willy-nilly she had come with her son to such a place with a burden of grudge, grouse and anguish.

About a year had elapsed and he had gradually familiarized himself with the environment and had learnt working knowledge of the local language. He was getting help of some local men to search for new species and plant fossils. In addition to his normal routine office work he was giving more of his personal time in his quest and his mother was continuously finding herself alone & solitary but she had no way out and was feeling herself to be a captive, though she very well knew that her son was behaving that way to remain out of the shock of missing Malini. She remembered of the fateful day when in the evening her son came with a packet of sweets and touching her feet said,

"Mummy, I have passed M.Sc. in first division and if you bless I would like to go for doctoral research in the botany department."

"I am very happy my son. All my blessings are with you. Whatever you want you do, I will never stop but only thing you do for me is that you marry and let me have company of my kids in the house. You see I have been bringing you up all alone ever since

your father died and now I feel fed up of my loneliness."

"In fact I wanted to tell you something but I was afraid of and could not gather courage to tell you."

"Don't worry. I am myself asking you, if you have somebody in your mind don't hesitate tell me frankly otherwise I will find out a suitable girl for you from my community."

"I am in love with a girl for the last over five years and like to marry her but she is not from our community and that's why I could not tell you."

"Who is she and what is her background?"

"Her father has been a senior inspector of schools in the state government and she has been with me right from the higher secondary onwards. I feel she also likes me equally but we have always maintained ethical distance as taught by you. She has

also stood first in M.Sc. and has a bright future."

"Will her parents agree to this marriage?"

"That I can't say but if you agree, I can find out from her and if need be meet her parents."

"So, still you have to cross that stage."

"Though I Know she loves me but I never asked about all this".

"Then why are you asking for my consent? First get preliminaries cleared but irrespective of that I would like to meet her. Can you bring her to me or arrange a meeting somewhere? I want to see her."

"Ok. I will try to bring her to you."

After a week, one afternoon he came to his house along with a girl clad in a light colored saree and blouse wearing a

Chappal which was simple but very sober. Though wearing simple attire, she was looking very graceful and alluring with a seducing charm.

He rang the bell and waited for his mother to open the door. As she opened the door, she was astonished to see a beautiful girl standing with Mridul. She could immediately guess that the girl was no other than Malini but without expressing anything she welcomed them inside. The girl touched her feet and politely entered the house. She took them to a small room where sofa and chairs were kept, which looked like living room and asked her to sit.

She went inside the house and after a few minutes called him to come to her. After another ten minutes Mridul and she came back with a tray containing glasses of water, some eatables and cups of tea. She offered Malini a glass of water and thereafter eatables and tea. While they were busy in munching savories and sipping tea, mother spoke,

"I understand you are Malini, is it not?"

"Yes Mummy I am Malini."

"Mridul has been speaking so much about you and I find you are really beautiful and polite too."

"It is your kindness Mummy."

"How long you and Mridul have been studying together?"

"From the higher secondary itself."

"Oh my God! For such a long time. Did you not fight with each other during all this period?"

Malini smiled at this question, just looking towards Mridul and then looking towards Mummy simply replied,

"We have been just friends and not husband and wife to fight with each other."

This was the turn of Mummy to smile. Though she used to look very serious and possibly that had become her nature ever since Mridul's father had died and all the responsibilities had fallen upon her shoulders when she was reasonably young. She just smiled with her lips getting widened and a bright shine coming in her eyes. She simply said,

"Ok, ok, I understand. But would you like to marry Mridul."

"As regards myself I am ready but we need blessings of parents of both the sides."

"What about your parents? I hope you have both of them."

"Yes, with God's grace both of them are alive. I don't see any problem with mother. She loves me too much and will agree to

whatever I say but problem may be with my father. He is a very stubborn person and if something comes to his mind, he does not listen to anybody. But I hope to get his consent."

"Ok. You are acceptable from my side and once your parents clear the proposal we can immediately go ahead with marriage preparations but what about your further studies and career?"

"I want to join research in botany and probably Mridul also likes that. That we can do as married persons also and in the meantime if some reasonable job is available that can be considered, however, all that will depend on the circumstances and also as you advise."

"Ok. Very good idea. Your thinking is welcome."

Mridul's mother was highly impressed with

Malini and for some more times discussions continued on topics of common interest.

"What are your plans ahead?" Asked the mother.
"I am here for a week more. I want to have some discussions with the professor under whose guidance I am planning for research work, apply for enrolment in Ph.D., apply for some fellowship and then go to my parents. I will first talk to my mother and she would, in turn, discuss with my father about the marriage. I hope within a month message will be conveyed to you."

"Oh, very good. May God bless you."

More than half an hour's time had elapsed that Malini humbly expressed her desire to go back. Mother asked Mridul to escort her to the main road and see that she got a proper transport. Though meeting was very short but Malini had won the heart of the Mother who in turn had started dreaming of the day when she would get the bride daughter-in-law in form of Malini. After ten days he told her that Malini having completed all formalities regarding her joining research work had left for her parent's place.

Mridul had also completed all formalities for joining doctorate research, however, under a different professor who was a renowned personality in the field of paleobotany and was well known for his work in finding out several extinct rare species of plants and their fossils. Mridul was very keen in searching for something which were hitherto unknown but might have existed in the remote past and that had aroused his interest in paleobotany. Pending his enrolment, he had started his work of literature survey and preparing synopsis of the proposed research work while hoping every day that some message might be coming from Malini. Equally eagerly was awaiting his mother for some message from Malini but as the end of month was approaching her anxiety was rising up and up and when they found that the month had elapsed and yet there was no message; that disturbed them immensely.

A couple of months passed by with so many bizarre thoughts of having Malini fallen in some trouble or having fallen sick or something abnormal might have happened in her family but yet nothing was heard from her side. The anxiety of both son and mother had gone sky high but no soothing drop of message rain was in sight. The mother had become restive and the son going hysterical losing his charm in research work and the normal life. In this condition a few days more passed by.

And lo! one day the lightening thunder struck and a bolt from the blue fell, when he heard a colleague in the botany department who was likely to join research under some other professor saying that Malini's marriage had been solemnized a couple of weeks back and he had seen the invitation card at one of his relative's house who was known to the groom and he only apprised him that her groom was a senior lecturer in a post graduate college near her home town and was quite elderly to her.

Still Mridul could not believe that news to be correct and thought that Malini would be coming to join research and only then the truth would come out. However, days, weeks and months passed by and Malini did not turn up to join the research work. The professor who was to guide her research work had also got worried of her not coming to the department and asked some of his research scholars to find out the reason and after a few days he got some heresay news that she had got married and had gone with her husband.

In a state of dilemma and shock he helplessly started his research work and decided to face the life the way it came. When his mother came to know of this she was taken aback and terribly shocked and was not able to reconcile herself that a girl who had gone so far off to marry his son and be her daughter-in-law had clandestinely married with somebody else and disappeared ignominiously sacrificing a career which was waiting her to take to greater heights.

With every passing day the chances of Malini coming back to his life was fading away and the effect of which were writ large on his face & behavior which was not hidden to the mother. One late evening he was sitting alone in the balcony, though it was becoming dark but he did not switch on the bulb. His mother came and asked,

"How long will you continue like this, what is that which is eating you away?"

Although both of them knew the reason behind that but still she liked to ask him to start some discussion with her son.

"No, no nothing. I am not able to pick up the thread of my work and my professor is busy with those scholars whose doctorate work is on the verge of completion and as such

he has no time to guide me. That is why I am a little worried."

"Is it that serious matter to be worried like this?"

"No, not that serious but I want to keep myself busy and complete my work in the minimum possible time."

"Normally, how much time does it take to complete the work and get the degree?"

"Three years to five years. I want to complete the things in three years and then go away."

"I hope you will get the research fellowship which can continue for four years then why are you in such a great hurry?"

"I want to go away from this place at the earliest as the place is now haunting me."

"You tell me that. Now I can understand what is haunting you but why don't you accept the facts of life and adjust yourself accordingly. When God closes one door, He opens another. Forget of the past and look for future, may be something better could be there in the store of time."

"Mummy, why are you befooling yourself? I know Malini's memories are haunting you more than they do to me."

"I don't deny that but what can I do and I cannot allow you to become Devdas."

"No, I won't do that but I will also not be able to reconcile and possibly I may never think of allowing any other girl in my life."

"Leave that to time and try to live in present with the truth of present. I will take care of you and you have to look after me as I am growing old & weak every passing day. I had plenty of thorns in my life and have survived only for you. I know your pains but

I want you to be a bold and forward looking person who takes good lessons of past. I like you to regularly read Shrimad Bhagwat Geeta and try to make yourself bold & above the realm of pleasure & pains."

"Ok, ok as you wish but be sure, whatsoever may befall I will never let you down."

The platonic love of mother always binds her sincere child.

CHAPTER – IV

Surprise

One day he returned home very late. It was around nine in the night. While coming back he was quite worried about mother and was also apprehensive that mother would rebuke him badly for having left her alone for such a long period of time. With frightened mind he ventured to press the call bell switch at the entrance door. There was no response for a couple of minutes which enhanced his fears of mother being terribly disturbed. He somehow gathered courage and rang the door-bell again. There was a loud voice,

"Can't you wait for a minute. Door is being opened."

He fearfully paused for another couple of minutes and then heard the sound of footsteps coming towards the door. Keeping his breath inside, he waited for the door to be opened. He heard the sound of latch being moved and then door being opened. As the door got opened he was surprised to see a beautiful young woman having opened the door and also heard the voice of mother coming from kitchen,

"Don't worry she is Meghna, come inside. I am a little busy in the kitchen."

He was surprised to see an unknown young lady in the house and was also taken aback to find his mother in the kitchen at such an odd hour. Normally she used to finish off all cooking by seven thirty in the evening and thereafter would be watching some program on the TV and only after his having come back she would get up to move to the kitchen to warm up the food and once he had freshened up both will come to dining table and take food together. After dinner gets over she would enquire about day's happening and about his next day's program and they would go to the bed or if she had any program of her liking would continue watching TV for another hour or so. During that time, he would be reading some book and thereafter they would go to the bed.

"Who is this woman Meghna?"

He wanted to ask his mother but could not gather courage to ask her and he simply liked to wait and see, if mother on her own told something about Meghna. He got himself quickly freshened up and they all assembled for the dinner. Mother and Meghna both brought the food items and placed them on the dining table and they occupied their respective chairs. Mridul was pleasantly surprised to see several items of his choice but he was hesitant to open his mouth in presence of an unknown woman and therefore without any ado started taking the meals.

"See, we have made several items of your choice, which one do you like most, just taste them all and tell me."

"But, tell me what has made you to prepare all these items. Now I have got accustomed of being happy with whatever you cook. As I know there is no festival to day and also I don't remember of any other occasion then why such a feast?"

"I felt like having a feast and without waiting for an occasion of festivity I have made this day an occasion. You only taste and tell me."

"Ok, ok. Let me try each dish but you both also start taking your food, I will tell about each item as I taste."

Mridul went on tasting every dish one by one taking small amounts and relishing them. Taste of a sweet dish was so good that he tried several times to ascertain that to be tasting best and accordingly he conveyed his mother.

"You have made me this dish several times and I am fully familiar with its taste but to-day its taste is different and that is really awesome. What have you done special today?"

"Why only this dish, you taste others also?"

"I am tasting others also. No doubt there is some difference but this one being quite familiar has attracted me most. Now please tell me what have you done?"

"That dish? See, today I have not prepared that. In fact, I only instructed and Meghna has prepared that. So you have liked that most. Oh, wonderful."

Mridul had no way out but to be silent and he could only speak,

"No, no I did not mean something. Every dish is equally tasty but can you tell me something about your new friend Meghna?"

"Not today. You only watch and wait. She is in need of some help and I am extending that to her and she is affectionately reciprocating."

Dinner was over. Mridul got up, went to the wash basin, cleaned his hands and mouth and then liked to go to his bed room. Mother and Meghna assembled all the utensils from the dining table and went to the kitchen to clean them up and wind up. He did not enquire anything as to how both the ladies were going to sleep but he could guess that mother would make some arrangement in her bed room for Meghna.

Next morning, he got up as usual at five thirty hours and moved towards kitchen, however, found that Meghna had already got up and was busy in the kitchen preparing bed tea. In fact, it was his duty to get up early, go to kitchen, prepare bed tea and then come to mother's bed room and ask her to get up but that day he had no scope for that. He could also observe that she had already taken bath and was wearing one of the old sarees of his mother. The house had three toilets & bath rooms, two attached with two bed rooms and the third one attached with living room which was very infrequently used only when visitors were there and possibly Meghna would have used that and might be mother had given her some clothing in the night itself. He patiently waited outside the kitchen and after a few minutes Meghna brought a big cup of tea and offered that to him. She placed a tea pot full of tea and two cups in a tray and went to mother's room. He went to his bed room with the tea cup to take his tea and did not like to disturb the ladies. He got busy in his daily routine and felt that here after he had nothing to worry for mother.

At nine hours he came fully ready to the dining table for breakfast and surprisingly found mother also ready having finished her bath. He was amazed with the change as mother would get everything ready before he left for office and only thereafter would devote time for herself. Meghna brought a number of items for breakfast, fried eggs, aloo paratha, sweetened curd and milk etc. of his choice. Mother wanted Meghna also to join them but she humbly declined. He and mother both took breakfast together and then he took his bag and car key to proceed to the office.

"Mridul, you come home early in the evening, we like to go the market."

"But why?"

"I like to purchase some clothing and other items for Meghna."

"Why, is she not having anything with her?"

"Yes. She is not having anything with her. With a lot of difficulties, she has been able to save her life and now she is all alone and devoid of anything. I have already told you that I am helping her."

"But why are you helping her. Do you know something about her?"

"Yes, I have come to know much about her and have seen her plight."

"Ok. If you want, I will come."

He came back home by four thirty in the evening. It was time for mother to be surprised that there was no time fixed for him to come back home and even whenever she asked him to come early he never came before seven in the evening. She remembered only one occasion when he had come before six evening but on that day he was totally unwell and needed to consult a doctor. She asked Meghna to prepare coffee and get ready to go to market. They took coffee with biscuits but Meghna was quite hesitant to accompany them and did not like something being purchased for her but mother did not listen anything and forcefully asked her to accompany. They went to a big cloth store and mother purchased a number of sarees and other items necessary for a young lady.

"Why are you spending so much for me, your help to save my life itself is much precious?"

"You keep mum. Let me do whatever I like." Said mother.

"I have never seen my mother for last so many years so happily marketing, so please let her do whatever she is doing." This was the turn of Mridul to speak.

"But I am totally an unknown person then why spending so much for me?"

"It is my mother's delight. She has seen only pains and pains in her life and I can do anything to see her happy,"

Mridul was surprised to have spoken those words to a beautiful young lady whom he did not know of but an inner urge had forced him to utter such a sentence. Mother seemed to be on shopping spree and went to some other stores & purchased a number of eatables and several other items. Once purchasing was over she liked to have some food in a restaurant and then come back home. This was totally unusual that many times he had requested her to take something outside just to give her a little relief from routine and for a change but she had always declined and see, that day she herself had asked to take food outside.

"Really something unusual and surprising," thought Mridul but one thing which was surprising him was why was mother behaving like that.

"Is something going to happen abnormal or unimagined?"

That thought flashed into his mind and he got totally perturbed. He had heard from the childhood days that extreme happiness was also indicator that possibly a person was going to complete his/her life's journey. But he kept cool and went on obeying the mother's wishes and mentally preparing himself to face the worst if at all that came but suddenly another thought came to his mind,

"If something really happened to mother, then what to do of Meghna?"

And that thought really disturbed him and shook him from inside and he could not think of any alternative to face a situation like that and still deeply immersed in that thought he took whatever food items mother had ordered in the restaurant without visibly showing any signs of worry. Having finished the sumptuous dinner, they drove back home; mother happily, Mridul worried and Meghna expressionless.

The next dawn came and the scene of previous day was repeated. Meghna had taken over the reins of the household and things were going on smoothly with clear signs of happiness on the face of mother but Mridul was not that happy rather he was worried to know about Meghna and how had she reached mother and was she really a genuine person deserving help or something else was there not visible to him and the mother.

A week passed by and the house hold routine had got practically stabilized with some good dish being prepared every day for the dinner. It was Sunday and every member of the family was in a leisure mood. A sumptuous breakfast had been finished by all the three members and Mridul had asked for a light lunch as he was planning to take family out for dinner. He and mother both were relaxing in easy chairs in the lawn while Meghna was busy in the kitchen doing something for the lunch.

"Mummy, you have not told me details about Meghna. Who is she and how has she reached you and why are you showing so much of affection and trust in her?"

"I knew, these questions would be haunting you and I am really surprised that you have contained yourself for a week. Ok, I will tell you something and rest Meghna herself will tell us."

"What is that, tell me."

"On that day it was two in the afternoon and I was standing at the main door waiting for the vegetable vendor. He was nowhere in sight that suddenly I heard a screaming sound and saw a young lady running helter-skelter and two bearded men chasing her. Nobody else was visible in the street and she appeared quite fearful & tired. As she saw me, she pulled up all her energy and

rushed towards me, requesting me for help and save her life. I don't know what really inspired me that I got attracted towards her and asked her to come and hide behind me. In the meantime, the two men chasing her saw her hiding behind me and came running to me asking to release her for them but I told them that she was my daughter's friend and if they created any problem, immediately police would be called and they would be handed over to them. This acted upon them instantly, they asked me for pardon and went away. I asked her to tell of her plight and she narrated me a pathetic story of having escaped from East Pakistan having lost her parents & other relatives and was trying to save her life. I believed her story and have given her shelter. I am confident my belief won't betray me. It is better some day you yourself ask her of the truth and if feel like you can verify that."

"Ok. Let me see carefully for a few days more. But what is her full name and something more about her."

"She is Meghna Sanyal and her father was a professor in Dacca University. She told me that and also that she was teaching somewhere."

"Ok, ok. Let me see. I will myself enquire one day."

They had light lunch of some rice and curry and went outside in the evening to see an exhibition arranged by the army officials to explain people of happenings in the East Pakistan and their effect on our country, the problems of refugees, rescue & relief operations being conducted by army etc. and there from they went to a restaurant for dinner.

A mother easily believes whatever a daughter like lady tells.

CHAPTER V

Fate Changes

"*I* am Meghna Sanyal. My father Dr. Prafulla Kumar Sanyal was a professor of linguistics in the Dacca University. I am post graduate and doctorate in psychology and was a lecturer in a post graduate college at Dacca. My younger brother who was junior to me by five years did his doctorate in literature and was to go abroad for higher studies. We had a very nice family life. My mother though a house wife was a very good singer and always liked to recite compositions of great poet Kazi Nazrul Islam and was a regular invitee of all important concerts and such programs. Though things appeared calm & quite but a wind of freedom was sweeping across the country and people were smouldering to be free from West Pakistan. There was no feeling of Hindu and Muslim and all communities were in perfect harmony that suddenly the army from West Pakistan entered the arena and started massacre of all those whom they doubted and they unleashed a reign of terror on Hindus. Local Muslim population was standing with us and we had no apprehension and continued with our usual life. One night those brutes started massacre of innocent people in our locality. Some of our neighbor came and asked us to flee towards Indian borders. Whatever we could take in huff & hurry we took and fled in our car to safety along with our neighbors. One contingent of army men who was standing on the way after we had travelled for over hundred kilometers sensed our escape and chased us. We abandoned our vehicle and ran on our own. It was darkness of the night and the terrain was also hostile. We could not maintain our togetherness and went on running and running. Everybody was more concerned of his / her own life. By early morning I could notice that none of my family members were in sight and only a couple of neighbors were there with me. We tried to enter indian territory and somehow entered therein. We all went in different directions. After running for a few miles I reached a relief camp where some Indian soldiers welcomed me and looked after care & custody of all such people who had crossed the border to save their lives. I registered with them details of my parents and brother to know about them. Days were passing and my worries were increasing about my family members. After a few days some more people came to the camp. They recognized me and only they informed me that my parents and brother had been killed by the Pakistani army. Heavens had fallen upon me and I went hysterical but enough care was taken of me and gradually I regained myself and mentally got ready to face whatever came on the way. A period of about two months had passed and efforts were on to locate some of my relatives from

Chittagong, our native place to rehabilitate me but nothing came through. While in the camp I noticed that some Indian Muslims had been keeping an eye on me, possibly they were nurturing some ill intentions towards me. After a couple of months, I heard that war had broken out and Indian soldiers looking after our camp moved to East Pakistan leaving our care and custody on local people. One night muslims who were keeping their eyes on me entered the camp and tried to kidnap me. Fortunately, I got awakened and ran for my life. I called many people for help but nobody came forward. To prudence of my luck, Mummy saw my plight and saved me. This is in nut shell my story. I would be grateful if you can help me to locate if any one of my parents is alive and also can find out the truth of my story."

Meghna narrated her story when after over a month of her stay, Mridul enquired of her plight and he was taken askance when she asked him to verify her details and to that very politely he said that,

"In fact I have not even an iota of doubt on what you say and the way you have been behaving and mixing with us we had already guessed that you are from a good family but my main motive was to see if I could be of any help to you."

"Thank you. In case you feel I could be a burden, please help me reach any relief camp."

"No, no. I never meant that. You are most welcome to be with us. In fact, you have changed the life of my mother for which I stand grateful to you."

The lurking truth was that Mridul had developed a liking, a soft corner for her and possibly somewhere he was searching for Malini in her but he never liked to disclose that and a similar feeling mother was also developing towards her but she was hesitant to speak something to Mridul as it was too early to express any such feeling.

A couple of months passed by with the family life continuing with some ups & downs. The liberation war was over and a new country Bangladesh had come into existence and people from relief camps who wanted to go back were being repatriated by Indian authorities, however, Meghna had neither expressed any desire to go back nor any of her relatives had been located. Mridul had utilized his official channel to find out of what all she had narrated, however, without giving any inkling to her. After another month he came to know through Indian embassy that what all she had narrated was total truth. This acted as an enthusiasm booster and he became confident that she was a genuine lady.

"Shall I try to get back duplicate copies of all your certificates and degrees from the university of Dacca,"

"I would be grateful. Please also approach them to give me an experience certificate to enable me find some livelihood here."

"But why are you worried for that; is there any problem that you find with us."

Mridul spoke spontaneously but immediately he realized that such a question was neither called for nor reasonable as she was still an outsider refugee for them. Something transpired to the mother and she simply said,

"if any one of your parents or close relatives are alive and they could be located, you are free to take your decision to go with them otherwise be here till I am alive. You will not have any problem. In case you like to get some job for yourself that also we will try once your documents are received."

"You have given me shelter and treated me like your daughter, I will be with you as long as God willing but still I must be in a position to sustain myself."

"Ok. Don't worry for that."

A time period of six months had passed by and things were moving very happily & smoothly. Meghna had taken over the reins of house-hold activities and mother was totally free of burden. Mridul had also started taking lunch box with him and had stopped taking food from the office canteen. He had got his promotion and had become in-charge of the office. Though he had been given an option to move on transfer to a soft station but he had declined that and had liked to continue at the same station. One of his friends had helped to recover the duplicate copies of some degrees of Meghna which had given her confidence of getting a job if needed but she had got so much so involved with the happiness of mother that she had abandoned the thought of joining a job and was quite satisfied with the life the way it was going on.

Though Mridul had developed a soft corner for her and liked to have her as his life partner but was not sanguine what did she want and possibly mother had also seen her as perfect replacement of Malini.

One Sunday afternoon when Meghna was busy with laundry machine cleaning the house-hold linen and he & mother were relaxing in the balcony suddenly mother interrupted,

"My son more than five years have gone ever since we are here in this station and things of past have become past, why don't you think of starting your normal life afresh and also unburden me from that worry. In fact, I want to see my grand-children & play with them before my call comes from heavens."

"I fully appreciate your feelings and like to start a new chapter. Malini must be having her own life, why should I unnecessarily waste my life for her. In fact, I have

practically forgotten the things but whom to choose to replace her. Are you having someone in your mind?"

"Yes. I am having my eyes on one such partner for you."

"Who is that?"

"I understand you know of her. I have seen a flicker in your eyes. Why do you hide that from me?"

"No, no. You tell me of your choice."

"Why go far away, Meghna. I like her and she is also fully adjusted with us. I find you also like her. Is it not so?"

"You are right. She is a good lady and is fully mixed with us. Moreover, she is highly qualified and of course she will also have a support for life but I don't know, what does she want?"

"Leave that to me. I will do the rest."

"Ok. Then do whatever you like."

Though mother spoke that spontaneously but she knew that she was not having any idea of the mind of Meghna on that issue; yet she decided to thrash out the issue and felt sanguine to obtain the consent of the young lady. A couple of days passed by and one day it so happened that some saffron robed person who was walking in the street begging for alms happened to come to their house. Standing outside the door, he called for the house-lady to come out and help him. Mother and Meghna both came to the door and opened that at the same time. He looked at both the ladies and gazed them from top to toe one by one and smilingly said,

"O mother, this young lady is going to be your daughter-in-law very soon and will always keep you happy and satisfied. This is what is written on her forehead but as I

can see her parents would not be there to solemnize the marriage."

Mother asked Meghna to go inside and bring some edibles to give that to him but he again smiled and said,

"Possibly I was in this street only for this purpose. My job is over and now I don't want anything."

Saying that he went away without listening anything from her. That prophecy brought an internal joy to the mother as she has had been dreaming of seeing Meghna as her son's bride for several months and also gave her strength to put forth her proposal to Meghna.

"That saffron clad man that day roaming in the street had foretold you to be my daughter-in-law. Do you think such a prophecy has any relevance?"

Mother asked Meghna one afternoon when both the ladies were sitting in the verandah after having lunch, and Meghna was reciting some poem of Rabindranath Nath Tagore.

"I don't know. I don't believe in all such things. While I was a college student, one day a NAZOOMI (fortune teller) had come to our house and was examining each member of the family. He was telling so many things about every one of us which I don't remember but seeing me he had predicted a very happy family life for me and see to-day I have no family."

"May be you are right but don't forget that for a girl family means she herself, her husband, her children and may be parents of her husband. So still you have to wait and see."

Before she could react to mother's saying, mother quickly added,

"Do you like to have your own settled family life?"

"Why not; every girl likes that but I can't even imagine, what is there in my destiny. I have lost everything in my life and don't know what can happen to-morrow?"

"Though I appreciate your feelings and accept that whatever happened to you, was beyond your control but I feel if some opportunity looms large you are the master of your destiny. Only that you must identify the opportunity and grab it keeping Lord as the witness."

"But where is that opportunity?"

"My daughter, opportunity is knocking at your doors."

"Please clarify me, what do you want to say?"

"Let me be very frank. My son Mridul and you both are in the similar age group, both of you are highly qualified and you both have observed each other for several

months. *Will you consider my proposal to marry my son? I am confident you both can have a good family life and also keep me happy and satisfied.*"

"*But, you see I am totally an orphan a fellow forlorn, will he like to marry me?*"

"*That you leave to me, you simply give me your consent?*"

"*But please check the other side also when you are going to take such a major decision.*"

"*That is for me to check.*"

"*If God willing, let it be so.*"

Mother felt very delighted but without giving further expression she kept it to her mind and liked to wait for proper moment. But from next day onwards she noticed a little change in the behavior of Meghna, as she appeared to study the habits and likes &

dislikes of Mridul though very carefully; which only an experienced lady could have noticed.

Some days passed off without any change in the events with normal life going on as usual that on an auspicious day after having completed her Puja mother announced that,

"I have decided marriage of Mridul with Meghna and after a fortnight on the coming BEEHU festival day we will have their formal engagement. Accordingly all preparations will be made. Any objection from would be bride or groom?"

However, there was total silence.

A mother is the best judge of inner feelings of her children.

CHAPTER VI

<u>Help</u>

"*My* days are numbered and any day, any moment my strength to speak and to see you all may disappear. I like every one of you to be with me all the times but I know that is not possible. Let my grand-son, whenever, he is free to be with me. I want to give him maximum time available with me."

"No, no. You are coming back home. We can't live without you."

"Neither I have control over my end nor you can make me live beyond the time that is allotted to me by God."

"Whatever you may say, we won't listen. We want you to be with us. Now when you are having a happy life, why you talk of going away."

"What can I do? If I have to go, I will go. Only let me enjoy the company of every one of you, for whatever time is available to me."

Mother had been hospitalized ten days back for respiratory and some other problems and since then Mridul, Meghna and grand-son Amit were giving maximum possible time and attention to her during day time, however, Mridul used to be there whole night with her. Whenever she was in relaxed mood, she used to talk a lot particularly about his childhood, her days of struggle and about her grand-son who used to be with her for most of the times.

"Do you remember when your father died you had just passed your matric and we were left in a very bad state of things. All

relatives who had come to attend different ceremonies were not interested in our future but their only interest was to take maximum possible assets from us in name of family property."

"Yes, I very clearly remember. The thirteenth day, after the last rituals were over people took away from our house whatever they could get and went away to their homes leaving practically nothing for us."

"Those were very bad days. Your father had not left much money in his bank account and we had landed in too many difficulties to get that and also equally difficult was to get his terminal benefits."

"Mummy, I remember everything, how can I forget. We had nothing even for two ends meet and what all we had borrowed for funeral and other ceremonies that also we had to pay back."

He remembered the tough times that they had to face to carry on their life. On next day of the last ceremony all relatives had left and they had taken away with them whatever they liked, however, nobody had even the least courtesy to ask them how were they going to face the future. Mother and son both were in doldrums and nothing was in sight but mother had decided to stand strong and face the tough times. He went into the memory lanes,

"*Two days have gone and I have not been able to give you food except tea and have no money with me, what to do I am not able to think?*" *Expressed mother with deep anguish.*

"*If you permit me, I will go to my friend Ramesh and request him for some money. He is the only person who may help me but he can also help only a little.*"

"*No, that is not good. I won't like that. Let me check once again all my containers as I have a habit of keeping some money somewhere and forget that and suddenly some day I will find that."*

Mother went to the kitchen and started checking each and every container but there was nothing. Even the salt container was empty. Then she went to small store room located by the side of the kitchen and there she checked every container and vial. Alas! there also everything was empty. She was in deep sorrow but her eyes had gone dry. She was weeping & crying from inside but no tears to wet the eyes. She was ready to bear any pangs of hunger but how to see her son hungry and in that pitiable situation mother and son spent two days, however, with no help in sight. Mridul thought of doing some manual job to earn two ends meet but that was not acceptable to the mother. Finding no clue to tide over the situation she decided to sell away two beautiful gold bangles which her husband had presented to her on their twentieth wedding anniversary and those were the most precious treasure to her.

Mother and Mridul both went to the gold smith who was known to his father and she sold away those bangles with a very heavy heart. The gold smith was quite hesitant to purchase them as he himself had got them specially made but once she insisted, he had but to accept and and he paid them the most reasonable amount as per prevailing gold rate. As both came back home, the most sorrowful chapter of their life had already been written the imprint of which was going to be unforgettable.

"Mummy! the money that you have arranged by selling your bangles will suffice to pay our outstanding loan and may be our own expenses for a month but what shall we do after that? Said Mridul.

"God, is great. Don't worry my son. He will get us some way out. Only that let us be prepared to face any odd and the most

unexpected worst situation. If we stand solidly these days will also fly away remember tough times never last, tough people do."

"Month of July is not far off and I will have to take my admission in the higher secondary classes which would need a lot of money, where from will that come?"

"That worries me but I will not like any hinderance in your studies. I am ready to live hungry but I will see you studying."

"How will a son allow his mother going hungry. Then I will do something."

"Any way still more than two and half months are there. Let us see what is more in store for us."

Mridul's father was a teacher in the local degree college and had a very high reputation as an honest and sincere teacher. He was revered amongst students but a number of peers and the college principal did not like him as he never liked to indulge in undesirable activities and groupism which was prevalent amongst the teaching community. His honesty had threatened several of them indulged in serious corrupt activities and still many people had serious doubts about his sudden death but Mridul and his mother never thought on those lines and accepted his demise as an unfavorable act of fate to them and wanted to go ahead in their life without looking back and without raising any question mark on anyone. They had expected that college authorities would extend some help as per normal practice by way of offering compassionate appointment to his mother and releasing ex-gratia payment but nothing came forward and the principal or any one of the school management did not show any interest to help them. No doubt that evoked a sense of doubt of something being wrong but considering other repercussions they preferred to ignore that and rather concentrate on finding some way out for their future.

"My father was a highly reputed teacher of the college and students were respecting him most but so far none of his colleagues or college principal has come to us either to convey condolences or for extending any help to us, what could be the reason?"

"I have been observing their behavior quite carefully and of course that hurts me. Even the normal courtesy they have not shown so far which indicates that there may be some foul play or they might be working with some calculated intentions. No doubt, some persons have expressed their doubts about sudden death of your father but considering our helplessness and the attitude of relatives I want to face the impending circumstances silently and concentrate on building up your future."

"So, you mean we should not try to find out what could be the reason of my father's sudden death."

"I did not mean that. We must try to find out the truth and gradually time itself will tell the truth. Our problem is how to manage our living ahead. Whatever, amount of money we have managed can't support us beyond a month."

"Ok, let me also try to see if I can do something without disturbing my studies."

One day while roaming aimlessly in the nearby park, being totally lost in the anxiety of future he met one student of his father who was quite senior to him.

"I am extremely sorry that our Guru Ji has passed away, I was not aware of this. Only after coming here I came to know of it. I want to meet Mataji, can you take me to her?"

"Why not. Let us go."

Both of them left the park and marched towards the house of Mridul. It was Mani who had come to the college as a mediocre student and was very naughty. He always liked to tease teachers and was not interested in studies but was very good in sports and other activities. He belonged to an affluent family hailing from a near-by town and was extravagant. College teachers did not like him and most of the students also avoided him. One day he had fought with some students and was to be reprimanded by the Principal and at that stage Mridul's father had intervened and liked to examine the total train of events before some action was taken on him. During investigations he found that Mani was not at fault but because of his reputation he was being brought to book and he pleaded for him; as a consequence, action proposed against him was dropped. This had brought him close to father who continuously took care of him and guided him to become a good and responsible student. He did very well in the college and joined the university to become a graduate in commerce but after that he left his studies and concentrated on his family business but always maintained contact with his father and always respected his mother. But for several years Mani had neither visited them nor was in contact with them and his to-day's meeting was unexpected & rather surprising. As they reached the house Mani looked a bit disturbed and started moving behind Mridul who rang the door-bell. Mother opened the door and stood spell bound to see Mani standing behind Mridul. She greeted him with all love and affection and Mani also respecting her touched her both the feet immediately.

"I welcome you my son. But why did you not see us for so many years." She spoke to Mani with tears in her eyes.

"Mata Ji I am extremely sorry and I really feel pained to find Guru Ji having gone away from us for ever."

"That is true, but what to do. Any way you come inside and be comfortable."

Mani came inside the house along with Mridul and occupied a chair lying in the living room. Mridul went inside the house and brought a glass of water which Mani took in his right hand and drank. He preferred a dialogue with mother.

"Mata Ji once again I like to express my condolences but I like to know how Guru Ji died suddenly, what had happened to him?"

"Leave that issue. It is a fact that he is no more. I can only say that it is the will of God."

"I find that you and Bhai Mridul, look to be in very bad state of affairs. How do you plan for the future?"

"That is where we are stuck up and we are not able to find a way out. Let me see what does God want of us?"

"Mataji if you don't mind I would like to suggest something."

"You are also like my son. Whatever you have in mind tell us."

"We are having a junior college up to higher secondary level in our town run by a trust headed by my father. You join there as a teacher for any subject you like. Only thing that you may have to commute a distance of about ten kilometers every day and if you feel like I can arrange your accommodation near the school. This can solve your financial problem."

"Your suggestion is acceptable to me. It is just like a drop of rain on a dry & perched soil. But what do I do."

"You simply make out an application addressed to the School Principal and give that to me. Within a week's time you will receive a formal appointment letter and then you join as soon as possible or otherwise after getting the letter you ring me and I will myself come and take you to the school for joining the job. Other formalities you can complete afterwards."

"Oh, thank you very much. To-day God has again come to my help and I have got convinced that 'as you sow as you reap,' is correct. My husband has helped many students who were reasonably good in studies but none of them has turned up to know about us but you, who was not having high reputation, are repaying the goodwill of your Guru."

"Mata ji once I have treated you like my mother, I will always be there to help you whenever you are in need. Forget the past, let us face the time which is with us. I know you are a person of self-esteem; it is the only respectful way to help you."

Mani asked mother if she wanted any immediate monetary help or anything else to which she declined. He took a written application from her and bade her good bye and went away. After a week she received through post an appointment letter as a lecturer of English for teaching middle level classes. The emoluments and the service conditions were quite reasonable tempting her to join without delay. She rang Mani and expressed her gratitude for such a timely help when nobody was around her. He asked her to wait for a couple of days when he himself would come and take her to school for joining the new assignment. Though summer vacation was approaching yet she was allowed to join which she did thanking God! Almighty for His mercy & benevolence.

A new chapter, a new life started for her. Though teaching was not something new for her as she was a postgraduate with required qualification of teacher's training and was a lecturer in a higher secondary college before her marriage, but that life she had already left over two decades ago. When her marriage was being settled with Mridul's father, her inlaws had put a condition that she would become a house wife and would fully devote looking after family chores. Her father was not agreeable to that proposal but she was so impressed with Mridul's father that she herself came forward and accepted the condition however, she had suggested that if adverse circumstances arose she would join a job to support the family and lo! after two decades of married life the unpleasant occasion had come. Mridul's grand-parents were big land lord having a big chunk of cultivated land and parental property in the ancestral village but Mridul's father was interested in academic life and after doing his post-graduation in Sanskrit he had joined the degree college in that town as a lecturer. The town was quite far off from the ancestral village and she had stayed with in-laws in the village. That situation had continued for over five years till in-laws were alive and once they left the world she had shifted to the town to live with Mridul's father where after a year Mridul was born. They got their house constructed in the town and settled there maintaining little contact with the village where his cousins were looking after the properties & cultivation and were occasionally giving a part of produce to them. But the situation in hand was totally different that all relatives had deserted them and the authorities of the school where Mridul's father had served for so long had also not taken care of them leaving mother and son in a lurch of helpless ness.

She had a tough life ahead. Every morning she would get up very early, finish off all house hold work, prepare breakfast & lunch for Mridul and her own tiffin, get herself ready by eight hours in the morning, quickly take her breakfast, pack her tiffin and after giving suitable instructions to him would move hurriedly to catch a bus to go to attend her duty at the school. She had to move a distance of about one furlong each way from her residence to bus stand and from bus stop to school every day. After coming back from school in the evening she would devote her time to look after her son, preparing dinner, other house hold activities and also check test/home work of the students. The initial first month was not that tough as home exams were approaching and teaching activities had come to low ebb, limited to guiding the students and completing syllabi wherever they were incomplete. The school exams continued for over a fortnight and then came the vacations, however, still she was required to attend the school for a couple of hours. Mani's father had advised Principal to take care of her so that she could settle down at the earliest possible and also to keep her reasonably busy to divert her attention from the agony she had.

"Ma'm I have heard enough of your husband; that he was a noble person and very popular in the student community. Did his college not come forward to help you?"

"He is past, and the present is that I am here serving with you."

"Is it your first teaching assignment."

"No. Before marriage I was teaching in a local college but that I left after marriage and after some years shifted to the present place where my husband had been serving."

"What are the subjects that you taught in your previous assignment."

"Being a post graduate in English literature, my first choice was English but in addition I used to teach mathematics also."

"Here what are the subjects that you can teach?"

"English to higher secondary classes and mathematics to junior classes. If need be I can teach Hindi also."

"Any special interest."

"I like Origami. If some students take interest I can devote some extra time for that, but that would be a purely non-paid assignment for the benefit of interested students."

"Oh that is excellent. Definitely we will take benefit of your art and skill. Let the vacations be over, from next academic session onwards we will start a session for that twice or thrice a week."

Principal was an old gentleman and liked to see that she started her new life and new assignment without any psychological trauma and he tried his best to indirectly help her. A month of service was over and she had received the first emolument. One day she went with a packet of assorted sweets to the house of Mani, met her parents and profusely thanked them for all the help to take her out of the tide. They also remembered the services of her husband to transform Mani into a brilliant student and a responsible person.

Mysterious are the ways of God, if He closes one door, He opens another.

CHAPTER VII

Flame goes off

$\mathcal{D}$ays were passing in company of Mridul, Meghna and grand-son Amit and nights were passing in sharing memories of days gone by in the company of son. Many saddest thoughts were giving the most melodious songs of time. A time span of twenty-five days had elapsed and condition of mother was fluctuating, sometimes improving and again sometimes dipping down. Doctors attending on her were doing their best but they were baffled with her fluctuating response to the medications. There appeared an improvement in her condition and doctors became hopeful to get her well soon. They could assess that after four to five days she would be alright and would be released from the hospital but that sudden improvement somehow, alarmed Mridul as he remembered his mother always saying that when flame of a lamp flickered brightest that was the time for that to get extinguished but he did not express his apprehensions to Meghna and got himself lost in the discussion which he was having with mother during night hours.

"My son, I very frequently see your father calling me as he has been feeling alone for all these years. Though he says he has all the comforts and is free of worries but loneliness torments him. I every time tell him about my happiness with my children and ask him to be happy, wherever he is but he insists on his demand."

She said one night to Mridul asking him what should she reply when his father called her next time,

"I have spent my life struggling in various ways when you were alive & were with me and also when you left me totally helpless. I had to fight even for my existence and only

now I have got some peace & happiness with my children; let me enjoy for some more days." Tell him that very clearly Mridul replied.

"Tomorrow, suppose, if I am not there, what will you do; how will you keep Meghna and Amit?"

"What silly thing are you asking Mummy? None of us likes to live without you."

"But that is universal fact of life that everybody has to die one day."

"Let us be together with you and let Amit enjoy your affection. Why do you want to deprive him of your affection, care and grooming?"

"I also like that but what can I do if my call comes from supreme authority."

"I can't win with you but only wish you continue living with us for some more time."

"My continuance or discontinuance depends on the will of God! But one thing remember, that my this mortal body will disappear in PANCH MAHABHOOTAS (Earth, Sky, Ether, Fire & Water) but parents never go away from their children. They remain close to them in form of invisible body and always look after them. If children are happy, they also feel happy and if children are in trouble, they feel extremely pained and therefore it becomes most sincere & sacred duty of children to keep their parents delighted in their invisible being. I hope you understand what I mean."

"Yes. I fully follow you and be sure I will never let you down whether you are in visible form as of to-day or you become invisible being."

"Thank you my son. Now I feel satisfied."

One morning doctor on round was very happy to see her condition and expressed to watch for a couple of days more up to coming Sunday and then release her for going back home. That was a very welcome news and Amit was extremely happy that he would be getting back the company of grand-mother. On Saturday evening she asked Meghna to prepare certain items of her choice and bring that next day for lunch. Though Doctor had advised her to avoid those heavy items but still she insisted and reluctantly Meghna agreed to her demand. While asking for those items Mother further added,

"So far I have been treating you like my daughter and daughter-in-law both but now I wish you become full-fledged daughter-in-law."

"But why so? I will remain your daughter and daughter-in-law both why do you want to change me so suddenly."

"See, a daughter always needs affection & support of mother but a daughter-in-law

can stand on her own feet. I have seen you as a very mature person who has experienced many hues & colors of life and you are fully fit to give affection and also bear all the burden."

"No, no. Excuse me don't make any change and let me be what I am."

"I like telling you because you can understand the pangs of pain. Mridul had a very sorrowful past and you have come in his life as a cool breeze. So you take care of him. Amit is a very charming boy, when he grows up always ensure that he concentrates on his aims & objects and help him become a good person. If he likes to go abroad, let him go."

"But why are you telling me all these things today. Everything will be done the way you want under your care & supervision, after all after a couple of days you are coming back home."

She laughed and said smilingly,

"I know and I know very well but still it is my duty."

After sometimes Meghna and Amit left the hospital to go back home but while on way Meghna was feeling disturbed as to why Mother was telling her to become a daughter-in-law alone. Was there something in her mind? She also thought that Mother was not so old to think of her death and then why all those bizarre thoughts had come to her mind? When Mridul came home to freshen up himself, take his dinner and also collect food for Mother, she asked him,

"See, Mother was telling me something in the hospital the context of which I could not understand. Will you tell me what she meant?"

"I heard something and am equally puzzled. I have seen her for so many years passing

through thick & thin of life but neither she appeared so happy nor speaking something like that. May be because of long sickness, she is wandering in the land of so many thoughts."

"Are you sure, it is the effect of sickness?"

"What else could be?"

"But that has surprised me. I wish she becomes normal and comes back home."

"Don't worry, keep cool."

Though Mridul was already disturbed from inside but he was advising her to be cool & composed, however, he knew that Meghna was not only attached to her but also felt her to be savior and liked to do anything for her and possibly she may not be able to withstand the untimely departure of mother but any way he also could only pray to God.

He came to hospital to stay with Mother for the night; having brought sweet preparations of her liking and offered to her. She took those eatables very happily and expressed her satisfaction on the sincere efforts of Meghna. That night she appeared to be in a talking mood and went on narrating many stories of her life to her son,

"Do you remember the most treacherous episode played by Mohan Kumar who was a colleague of your father and was known to be living alone away from his wife?"

"No. I only had heard his name."

"After having got settled one day I went to the college of your father, met his principal and requested him for settling his terminal benefits and provident fund etc. He asked me to formally apply and submit a number of supporting documents which involved running about here and there. By and by I started collecting them. One day Mohan Kumar met me in the college and voluntarily

offered his help. Willy-nilly I nodded for that hoping that he would genuinely help but instead of helping me he started flirting me and delaying my case further. It became a headache for me. In the evening when I would return back I would see him standing at the bus station waiting for me and there from he would accompany me up to the house saying in one way or the other that the world was not good for a widow and I should marry him. One day he crossed all the limits and tried to enter our house and when I resisted he threatened to see that how could I continue in the job and get my terminal benefits. In fact, he had become a nuisance and had made my life a hell. You were too young to understand & face him. Being fed up with his activities ultimately one day I called Mani in the college and narrated him the whole thing and he assured me to get everything settled. One day he came behind my bus in his own car and when he saw Mohan Kumar following me, he came there took Mohan Kumar by surprise and warned him that if he did not mend his ways he would have to face the consequences. He also went to the college principal and asked him in very clear terms to settle the case of terminal benefits quickly. His intervention worked miracles. Mohan Kumar thereafter never disturbed me and also all your father's dues were settled. In fact, I owe myself to Mani who had acted as my savior. I would also like that you stand indebted to him and if you could do something for him do that whenever opportunity arises."

"Ok Mummy. I shall abide by you but I don't know whether any such opportunity will come to me."

"Don't worry, you would have never expected sudden disappearance of Malini and unimagined coming of Meghna who is much better than her."

"Mummy, leave it. You have had been a devotee of Lord Krishna, please tell me something which will give me light in *darkness when you would not be there to guide me."*

"Every now and then I have been telling you many things but definitely I will tell you to-day something which you must remember. We are sent to this Earth by Lord for some purpose but we don't know that and get entangled in worldly deeds. Those who search their soul get to know something of their purpose and if they make efforts to achieve them, they become enlightened. We do many things with some attachment, some aim, some objective to achieve but we forget that we are mere tools in the hands of creator who is playing through us and how this game will proceed & where will it end only He knows. Our physical being which has come into existence through a beginning will end one day but this is just a part of an unending game of birth & death which is going on and will go on. We are here in the world for doing our KARMA without worrying for consequences just like a seed which grows but does not

bother what fruit it would bear. You are your own friend, you are own enemy and only you are responsible for your rise or downfall. Pleasure & pain are our own mental creations and one who rises above them can march to emancipation and the last thing that I like to tell you is that whatever good or bad one does, ultimately he gets back the same with compounded interest in this life time itself. That is all the essence of life that I have learnt through my life's experiences & studies and possibly that may be of some help or meaning to you and I hope you have already got a glimpse of same."

"Mummy your words, your teachings I will always remember. In fact, your life, your struggles, your spirit to stand steadfast even in the worst of situation itself has given me the lesson of life and your words spoken now will be probably the last gift of a mother to his son and the most powerful beacon light to me."

He found Mother feeling sleepy and therefore discontinued the discussions and allowed her to sleep and he also slept on the attendant's cot kept in that private ward. Next morning i.e. Sunday morning she got up little early and awakened him also. She went herself without his support to bath room and freshened herself. She completed her morning routine and liked to have some tea. Normally hospital tea used to come by seven O' clock morning and she used to complete her morning routine just by that time. He went outside and brought a cup of tea which she took happily and asked him to switch on the TV to watch news bulletin of Doordarshan. At the normal hospital time morning tea came which she took again sharing with him; and half an hour later duty Nurses came to give her a bath and change all the linen which was got completed swiftly within fifteen minutes during which period he remained outside the room and once Nurses went away he came in and found Mother looking very fresh. Breakfast came from the hospital canteen at eight hours which she took relishing and asked him to share a few pieces. It was time for him to go home informing the Nurses and placing call bell switch very close to her for calling any emergency help.

He came back around eleven hours accompanied by Meghna and Amit. They had brought several items of her choice and liked to offer her for eating but she desired to take them along with hospital lunch at twelve thirty hours. Meghna insisted her to take pomegranate juice which she took happily. She liked to play chess with Amit using the small chess board brought by him. Gradually game became very interesting, Mridul siding Amit and Meghna siding Mother. One & half hours passed by watching the game between two super heroes that the hospital canteen boy knocked, bringing in the lunch plate. All of them rearranged their positions. Mridul placed the lunch plate on the mobile platform and moved that properly so that she did not experience any problem in taking the food and Meghna went on giving small-small quantities of different items what all she had asked for last night. She enjoyed all the food items and after she had finished the meals Mridul got her mouth and hands wiped clean with tissue paper and shifted away the mobile platform and collected the lunch plate and placed that at a suitable place. Once mother had finished her ritual of taking medicines post lunch, Meghna, Mridul and Amit also sat together to have their tiffin and the items which had not been consumed by Mother.

A very happy environment was continuing all the four members of family happily chit-chatting and enjoying. Amit was most happy and expressing his feelings he said,

"Grand Ma I have been missing you in the nights for over a month, tomorrow onwards as you come back home I will be sleeping with you and will listen a lot of stories from you."

"Don't worry my child I will tell many stories as long as you want."

"Dadi, I have not heard from you the LOREY songs which I was told you used to sing to sleep me in the night, will you sing them to me."

"Definitely, any number of songs you want I will sing for you but many songs now I have forgotten."

Though Amit was over ten years old & studying in fifth standard but he used to behave as a young child with grand-mother and she always treated him most affectionately pouring on him all her love, care, concern and compassion. In fact, he was the life line of grand-mother and repose of her life. Amit also was so much so fond of Dadi that thinking of living without her was a nightmare.

It was around five hours in the evening a Nurse came to check her blood pressure and temperature and administer a dose of medication. She was astonished to find her blood pressure abnormally high and rushed to call a doctor to advise next course of action. The worry of Nurse caused a worry in Mridul and Meghna too but Amit could not understand why people were looking tense whereas mother was looking slightly restive and nothing beyond. Being a Sunday only one doctor was available that too he was in the causality ward. As he got the message he came running and seeing the rising blood pressure he also got alarmed. He thoroughly checked the entire case history and found only problems related with lungs, pneumonia, sinus and breathing trouble and of course age related problems. However, he suspected some cardiac problem and called for any available cardiac specialist of the hospital but none could be located. He advised her being shifted to intensive care unit (ICU)awaiting arrival of another specialist whom he called for from a nearby hospital. Family members were not allowed to enter

ICU which aggravated their anxiety experiencing every second passing as an era. After about twenty minutes the specialist from the other hospital came and went inside ICU to examine the mother. A few minute after he came out with a grim face and without talking to anybody went away. That was enough for Mridul to guess that something was seriously wrong.

After another five minutes the hospital Doctor came out of ICU and sorrowfully informed them that she had passed away due to massive cardiac arrest. Had it not been a Sunday probably she could have been saved.

Death lays its icy hands even on kings most unexpectedly.

CHAPTER - VIII

Happiness

The departure of beacon light had left behind an unending trail of sorrow and void. The house which was full of happiness had become a ghost house. Though every family member was searching for something but he was not clear what was he looking for. Days were passing, nights were passing, working weeks were passing, Sundays & holidays were passing but everything and everyone seemed moving as a machine part devoid of charm, enthusiasm and lacking element of energy. What a pal of gloom, which had enveloped everyone in the family. Mridul was as usual attending to office, Meghna was busy with house hold activities & taking care of her son, Amit was busy in attending the classes and doing his homework and also playing sometimes when his friends were coming to his house. Then why was the void?

From that fateful Sunday onwards the family was busy for next fifteen days in cremation and other funeral rights. Entire office of Mridul had come to their help and all those who knew family tried their best to help them and ensure that they don't feel any problem or deficiency of support. In fact, couple had felt extremely grateful for the help & support they had received in the hours of tragedy and need that Mridul was overwhelmed with the kindness, courtesy and support of the people of north east that he had totally forgotten he was in a land far away from his own place and possibly had he been in his own native place he would have never received such a support of acquaintances, staff and officers and friends. That had helped him overcome the loss of his divine mentor and Meghna had really proved an asset when the mother was alive and also when after she had departed to her heavenly abode. That was the period when he realized that his decision to come to north east and stay there was how much correct. Thank God for the wisdom that prevailed in him.

After a month had elapsed and gradually the things had got stabilized one evening while sitting in the balcony along with Meghna and watching the play of his son along with other children of his age and discussing about how mother had recognized the hidden traits of Meghna and had proposed him to marry her, he got reminded of the assurance given to Mother on the last night that he would never let her down and would remain happy to see that she stands delighted in her invisible form. He immediately said to his wife,

"I had given an assurance to Mummy that we will remain happy to see that wherever, you are you remain happy by our being

happy. Somehow I had forgotten that in her loss but our sorrow will not allow her to be happy & content."

"Oh my God! why did you not tell me that?"

"See, I had sunk so deep in sorrow that I could not remember anything what I used to discuss with her during night hours in the hospital."

"Will you tell me in brief important points that she told you so that we can fulfill her wishes?"

"Why not, without you I cannot do anything."

Mridul narrated in brief various points that she had told him particularly the tips of knowledge given on the last night. Many discussions were mainly regarding their own life & struggles about which he liked to share with her from time to time while sharing her experiences.

Next day onwards they made it a point to ensure that there was no element of sorrow in any nook & corner of their life and home as well. The change was so glaring that Amit could not resist to ask his mother about that,

"Mummy, what has happened that suddenly Papa and you both appear normal and happy and are doing your work enthusiastically? Something behind such a change."

"My dear son, parents don't really die, they only change their shape. Your Dadi who was with us all the times is still with us only that she has become invisible to us but she can see all of us. If we are unhappy she gets pained and therefore let us be happy to keep her happy."

"But we have burnt her off, then how can she see us?"

"That was the visible body what we call as mortal being, that body we have burnt off but your Dadi has acquired an invisible form and in that form she is always around us."

"Alright we cannot see her, but I must be able to feel her if she is around us."

"You are right and you can feel her also. Whenever you sincerely remember her, she will show her effect through some events or happenings but you need not worry for that and try to keep her happy wherever she might be."

"Ok, ok. I will not do anything wrong to cause pains to Dadi."

All the three family members were doing their best to ensure that Dadi was kept happy but still it was too difficult for Meghna to forget all the love, affection and care that she had received from her and now she was feeling all alone, an orphan, a forlorn and an individual without an identity. A period of five months passed by and gradually a stability had come to the family. Amit was in sixth standard and his half yearly exams were there at the anvil. Meghna was devoting more and more time towards his studies and exams and the grand Ma had become practically a part of daily ritual. Everybody in the morning after bath would go to her photo hung near the small sacred place of deities and pay obeisance to her along with prayers to other deities and then commence the day's work and thus practically Dadi had also become a part of deities.

Life flows unstopped with its melodies & bitternesses, ups & downs, twists & turns, waves & whirlpools and even in darkest of hours, makes its own path and goes ahead. Remembering mother and seeing Amit growing up & up five years had gone by and he was in Matric final year. Mridul had his further elevation and had become one of the very senior level officers of his organization with proposal to move out of north east office but he had again preferred to stay there and had been able to convince his bosses for the same.

Days, weeks and months were passing by and lo! the time of Amit's final exams approached and this time Mridul also became quite serious about him as after matric he had to move out to a boarding college for further studies and his performance was vital. Amit did very well in the exams and thereafter had a summer vacation of practically two months. Parents had so far concentrated on development of the child but they felt they should take him out and show various places of historical, cultural and religious interest and chalked out a program. Meghna had a long cherished desire to see UNAKOTI temples and KAMAKHYA SHAKTIPEETHAM and therefore they started their trip covering them first.

Mother, father and son, they started their journey on an auspicious Monday evening proceeding by train to Kumarghat station on Agartala-Lumding line in the north Tripura district. They reached there in the morning and proceeded by a car to Kailashahar, the headquarters of Unakoti district and stayed in the government guest house. After lunch they travelled in a car to the banks of river Mau where the famous Unakoti images and stone carvings are located in the foot hills of mount Unakoti. As they reached there they were mesmerized with the sight of great art scattered on the rocks & stones.

"Oh my God! what a wonderful sight, what a marvel carved into stones; unbelievable; a treasure of art and craft lying in such an unknown place." Exclaimed Meghna.

In fact, she was wonder struck to see a vast treasure of man-made art scattered in a picturesque forest location in the foot hills. Amongst the rock cut carvings she saw centrally located Shiva head and gigantic Ganesha figure, Goddess Durga riding over big lion, Nandi and thousands of figures, murals etc. of the Shiva cult. The central Shiva head known as Unakotiswara Kal Bhairava is about 30 feet high including an embroidered headdress which itself is 10 feet high. On each side of the head-dress of the central Shiva, there are two full size female figures - one of Durga standing on a lion and another female figure possibly of his consort Parvati on the other side. Amit was extremely curious to see all the figures and go around the place. Evening was approaching and yet a lot more was remaining and they decided to return back and come there again next day.

Next morning they got ready a little early, took packed lunch and came there along with a person who knew the place very well. He took them around to different locations, showed them almost all the images and carvings explaining the significance of each one. Place was having water falls but they had only trickle of water and the river Mau was also just a streak of water.

"Can you tell me who crafted these art work and what was the inspiration behind such a great work?" Amit asked the person accompanying them.

"There are many legends but nothing is known beyond doubt. All the stone images, carvings and murals have been built during seventh to ninth century AD and obviously different artisans would have made them. However, there is a very interesting legend that once Lord Shiva was going to Kashi along with one crore gods and goddesses including him, he made a night halt at this location. He asked all those accompanying him to wake up before sun rise and proceed onwards. However, in the morning, except him, no one else could get up so he set out for Kashi himself cursing the others to become stone images as a result we have one less than a crore stone images at this place."

"This country is really full of mysteries, histories and unexplored treasure and I feel

if one can know India, its culture and its known & unknown treasure, nothing more would be required to know of the mankind." spontaneously spoke Meghna.

"You are right. The more places you go and meet people, more you know of India and in fact one life time is too less to know fully this country, its people, its culture, its heritage, its hidden marvels and its history."

As the evening approached they returned back to the guest house fully hypnotized with the marvel they had explored and therefrom they came back home for the next sojourn.

Their next visit was to KAMAKHYA SHAKTIPEETHAM. A few days later they commenced their journey for KAMAKHYA temple in Guwahati, the capital city of Assam state. The grand temple complex is located in western Guwahati at the top of the Ninanchal hills at a height of 800 feet above the sea level and is one of the fifty -

two SHAKTIPEETHAM of Sati, the first wife of Lord Shiva. There is no image of Shakti there, however, within a corner of the middle cave in the temple, there is a sculptured image of the yoni (private parts) of the goddess, which is the object of reverence. A natural spring keeps the stone moist. Other temples on the Ninanchal Hill include those of Ten Mahavidyas (goddesses of great wisdom) like Kali, Tara, Shodashi, Bhuvaneshwari, Chhinnamasta, Bhairavi, Dhumavati, Bagalamukhi, Matangi, & Kamala and also goddess Ghantakarna etc.

The main temple has a beehive-like Shikhara (dome) with delightful sculptured panels and images of Ganesha and other Hindu Gods and Goddesses on the outside and consists of three major chambers. The western chamber is large and rectangular and is not used by general pilgrims for worship. The middle chamber is a square with a small idol of the Goddess, a later addition. The walls of this chamber contain sculpted images of Nara Narayana, related inscriptions and other gods.

Meghna had a long desire to see that temple from her child hood days and was overwhelmed to arrive at the shrine complex and Amit was curiously observing everything but Mridul looked stirred up as he had not been able to take his late mother to that shrine and she had left the world with an unfulfilled desire. Amit saw at a place a herd of goats, goat kids, a few male buffalo and buffalo calves and he could not resist his curiosity,

"Papa, what for these animals are herded here and also I see some people carrying he goats and goat kids tied with a rope around their neck?"

"These are meant for sacrifice."

"What is that?"

"KAMAKHYA is the biggest & most powerful goddess of mystic and tantric cult and these animals are slaughtered as sacrifice while performing such a puja."

"But goddess is mother, a mother is supposed to give & preserve life, how does she accept end of a life like that of innocent animals?"

"My son, you are right. I also don't like and believe in such practices but this is going on for hundreds of years and it is not easy to do away with this."

"Why. Why can't this be done?"

"My child, there are certain things which are deep rooted in public psyche and unless people change, they will continue."

"But when I grow, I will definitely raise a powerful voice against this practice."

"I like this attitude but how far you will succeed will depend on time."

"But what is this tantric puja, sometimes I have heard people speaking about this?"

"At this level of yours you understand in the simplest form that there are three types of pujas viz, Vedic pujas where deities are not there, only yajna/hawans are performed by highly knowledgeable priests with chanting of Vedic mantras and they are meant for universal good in limitless space of time; Normal pujas which are performed against deities with or without priests to invoke their blessings for good of individuals or a group of individuals in normal course of time and tantric Puja are performed by very special practitioners called tantric and are meant for achieving immediate objectives of an individual. Usually they are not for good purposes."

"Oh my God! why should a mother accept and encourage such things."

"People are having different motives, different objectives and different beliefs and accordingly they perform different types of Puja. In fact, mother goddess neither encourages nor discourages, it is only individuals who are motivated as per their needs."

"Is there any other type of Puja also."

"Yes those who are really enlightened, they don't believe in all such rituals. They see God everywhere and do meditation in solitude."

Mridul diverted the attention of his son from such a subject by telling him how the temple complex was built and the legends associated with that and they went to different temples and performed Puja in normal way. Whole day was lost and by evening they returned back to their place of stay. Next day onwards they proceeded to see the kingdom and historical treasure trove of great kings of Ahom dynasty who had ruled over north east for over six hundred years.

The vacations were coming to an end, the exam results were out and Amit had scored a very high percentage of marks standing top in the merit list of his school. It was time for him to get admitted in a college far away from parents in a prominent city. That was going to be another painful rendezvous for Meghna but willy-nilly that had to be done for the good of the future of her son.

Happiness arises from the bed of sorrows and asks for its own price.

CHAPTER – IX

The Agony

$\mathcal{T}$he days, the weeks, the months and years were passing and Amit was going up and up in the ladder of his academic achievements which was giving a new boost every time to the parents. Meghna finding herself alone throughout the day time had joined a coaching institute as a lecturer however that was a part time job and to fill that void she joined a non-government organization which was engaged in service of underprivileged people in far off villages. She experienced difficulties in going to distant places during half a day's time and therefore rearranged her coaching assignment to do three full days in a week and the rest of the days she was rendering her services to the unprivileged people in many ways.

The government accommodation where they were residing was very comfortable and full of amenities but ultimately one day Mridul was to superannuate from the government job. The couple dreaming of a peaceful life in the honored age and also having Amit and his family with them; they started constructing a big bungalow in a picturesque location which was having the beauty of her imagination and ingenuity. Sundays and other holidays were getting spent in the supervision of that house being constructed.

Amit was in final years of computer engineering at Indian Institute of Technology(IIT) Itanagar and had a plan to go abroad after completing that, whereas, parents liked him to start his own enterprise and be with them. however, it was left to time that would dictate the shape of things.

"Ever since you have come in my life, things have changed and I am also a happy person at home and performer in my department." Expressed Mridul one day when both of them were relaxing in lawn in front of the house.

"I don't know, how much have I done for you but the person who did for me, is always in my memory and every moment I feel her loss."

"That is with me also but I have made her memories and teachings as the source of inspiration and always seek her care & concern in you."

"Oh my God, so much faith in me."

"Do you know by this year end, I will get my last promotion to the senior administrative grade and people will pressurize me to move out, how do you feel?"

"No, I don't want. Either you forego your promotion or get this office upgraded to accommodate you at the senior most level. We are getting our house built here, what is the gain in moving out?"

"Ok, ok. Let me see. But suppose Amit does not like to stay here and goes abroad as he is thinking of."

"Even then I like to be here. After your retirement we both will serve the people and in addition you can continue with your research work. But unfortunately you never told me anything of what all you have discovered so far?"

"Yes, that is true. Our subjects have been so diverse that I kept you away from my work which is mostly connected with the identification and collection of fossil plants and also finding out newer species of plants which are hitherto unknown."

"Oh, certainly that would be very interesting. How many such plant fossils and newer species have you been able to find out?"

"Many. In fact, it is only my work under the pretext of which I am continuing here."

"Have you made publications?"

"Yes. Several publications in reputed journals and they have gone to the credit of myself as well as to botanical survey of India."

"Have you authored any book?"

"In fact I had no time but after my retirement I will be writing books on various findings and will seek your help in collating and compiling all the photographs."

"Oh, good; interesting so I have to understand the mind of plants in addition to understanding human behavior."

"You may take it like that."

Although Mridul's retirement was still over five years away but they had already started thinking on those lines and dreaming of a peaceful yet constructive life ahead. Though sometimes he remembered of his past, his child hood, his school days & his friends and of his native place but the present was so beautiful & benign that he felt himself contended with that. One Sunday while they were roaming in a park together and enjoying the chirping of birds nested there in the branches of big trees, Meghna suddenly asked,

"You know much of my past but you never shared anything of your past. Will you mind telling something of your struggles and strives?"

Mridul laughed to this and smilingly spoke, *"My present has been so melodious that I don't like to dwell in past and when I peep into them, they sometimes torment me. But*

I don't want to put cold water on your curiosity and therefore share my entire life till before your entrance in short and I presume my mother would have shared with you something how she had struggled to bring me up."

"Mother had shared with me so many things but her telling and your expressing something are different."

Mridul narrated many things of his past to Meghna and also how had he developed a liking for her but was hesitant to reveal that and how mother had recognized that which led to their marrying each other.

"Don't you remember Malini still, once upon a time she was your life?"

"That part of life is over; truth is in hand. Why to remember something which does not exist."

"I never see you normally going to any temple, why so?"

"I believe in God & goodness but don't believe in rituals. God or whom you call as supreme being is not an animate. All religions believe that God is omnipresent, omniscient, omnipotent and all-pervading then why to seek Him in shrines or temples. He is very much with us all the times."

"Then why did you like go to KAMAKHYA?"

"Any place is also vibrating with energy and whatever good or bad is done at a place, an imprint and effect becomes a part of those vibrations. As a consequence, some places give us peace & tranquility and at some places we feel agitated & disturbed. That is a sacred place, I liked to go there."

"My food habits are different than yours but you don't mind them, why?"

"It is our individual choice & preference. It is not food rather it is emotional understanding that makes difference."

"You have been in this region for very long, what are the things that you have observed?"

He again laughed and simply replied,
"It depends on beholder's eyes."

"Please tell me as a neutral, dispassionate person, what ails this region that can help me serve the people better?"

"This is a big question and there are many angles to this, however, as a normal person what all I have observed is that people of north-east are self-respecting having concern for their own identity & esteem and there are historical reasons behind that and after independence they have been thoroughly neglected by government at Delhi which has generated a feeling of alienation. They totally lack connectivity,

education, health care, transportation and also efforts have not been made for their absorption in the main stream of nation."

"Oh, my God, all the basic issues need be addressed but we will do, whatever, we can in respect of education of the people and advise on health care and empowerment of women."

Time had flown away and Amit had passed his final year and had got a fellowship for higher studies in the States. It was an occasion of mixed reactions. While son was getting his desires fulfilled, parents were feeling lost with many apprehensions but they never wanted to come on his way. All the formalities were completed and arrangements were made and ultimately in the last week of August Amit left his mother land on way to his dream destination leaving behind his mother and father having given him blessings & tearful adieu.

During first year Amit was very regular in contacting his parents through face time, Skype and WhatsApp but as years passed his contacts became less frequent but fortunately Mridul got his further elevation to the senior administrative grade and became regional director and head of all centers of his organization located in the north-east region which increased his travels to different offices. Meghna started devoting more and more time in visiting far off places, studying their problems and arranging programs for their upliftment. The infallible time went ahead unabated showing its own effects. Amit got an employment in Google at San Fransisco in California. He married a girl who was working with him and liked to settle there, which shattered the last iota of hopes which Meghna had so far kept somewhere in her heart that some day her son will come back and be with them.

The time had flown on its wings and the last year of Mridul's retirement from the service had approached. They had vacated the government accommodation and had shifted to their own bungalow. One Sunday afternoon sitting in their portico they were sharing their happiness and sorrows.

"I have had a wonderful life for thirty years with you and how such a long period of time has passed away is just like a dream."

"True and interestingly we never quarrelled with each other like other husbands and wives."

"It was purely due to you for having handled every situation very carefully."

"No. I believe it has been due to blessings of mother who has always been with us."

"You are right."

"What are you thinking of doing after your retirement?"

"As already said I will complete my books and then join with you in your social work."

"But our son is calling us to be with him. Why not we go there?

"You remember last time when we went there, despite our plan to stay there for three months, we stayed there only for two months and came back. Though all possible facilities were available and we had enjoyed the food in Google canteen also but we were finding ourselves to be fish out of water. We may go there from time to time for short spells of time but I don't like to stay there for long time and more over you are so much engrossed with your work that not worth giving that up."

"Ok. As you like it."

"Suppose if any one of us departs away from the world unexpectedly then what to do?"

"Where from such a silly thought has come to your mind. I don't like to think over such rubbish ideas. We both will go together. People have developed so much affection for us that even they will not accept any such thought."

"Sorry. I won't think of any more rubbish."

"But what about this bungalow and other assets?"

"Now it is clear that our son will not come back so we will donate everything to the organization you are attached with and let them do whatever good they can."

"That is a welcome suggestion and I stand by that."

The work load of Mridul had increased several folds and he had to travel outstation very frequently during which periods Meghna would plan her visits to far off interior locations. The population in such places were very thin and traveling in hilly terrain was very difficult and villages were also scattered in distant locations and several times insurgents were active in certain areas where her organization was avoiding sending any volunteer. On several occasions she had met with some hostile elements who had warned her not to enter their territory. She had been once deputed to an interior location where a couple of villages were reasonably close to each other but reaching there was very arduous & difficult as there was no proper road and on extremely poor pathways one had to travel through brooks & bushes, ups& downs of uneven hilly terrain, thorny vegetation and during rainy days those locations were full of hazards particularly of venomous creatures. She was conducting some programs under adult literacy scheme and also imparting awareness particularly to women folk for health & hygiene, family planning & childcare and also for empowerment of women through energizing local crafts, bamboo artwork and other traditional hand work.

It was the first week of June month sporadic rains had started. Mridul was having nine months more to superannuate in the ensuing month of March. He had been invited to attend some program at Delhi and being alone she had decided to stay overnight in one of those villages to complete her discourse and train ladies. Her aim was to avoid rainy season for such a difficult location. Sunday evening Mridul was to return back and accordingly She completed her work in the morning itself and started back around eleven hour's forenoon. Two village members accompanied her to reach up to make shift road where from a jeep of her organization would lift her up. It was a stretch of about two kilometers which was really very tough & hazardous and those two men were escorting her taking every possible care & precaution. While passing through very thick bushes, she moved ahead of them that suddenly there was a painful screech from her. Those two men immediately ran to her and were wonderstruck to see her bitten by a venomous snake and they saw the snake running away in the bushes. One of them immediately lifted her up and keeping her on his shoulders ran to the road and other one ran to locate someone in the dispensary which was about four kilometers away. As the man carrying her reached the road the jeep had not come till then. He got totally disturbed and became upset and like that ran carrying her towards the dispensary. Despite his best efforts it took about thirty-five minutes to reach the dispensary, where every possible effort was made to treat her but the venom had reached different vital body parts and unfortunately she succumbed. A lamp which was removing darkness of underprivileged people had got extinguished unceremoniously without being oiled by its mentor & humsafar (life partner).

Unexpected turns may be awaiting life at the zenith of its satisfaction.

EPILOGUE

"Oh my god! What have you done to me, I never doubted in You, I never left your hands; entire life I lived having total faith in You and in your justice; then why such an injustice to me; where will I go now; what shall I do; why did you take away my life from Me, what will I do with this body devoid of life?" Was the crying question Mridul was continuously asking God! Almighty.

But as usual God never replied to him, God never responded to him and probably God! did not listen to him and he had to face the holocaust himself alone.

His entire office, all the people known to the family and the people, wherever, she had been to serve the people, they all had gathered to bid her a tearful last adieu and for some days' people took care of Mridul but as the time passed by he was left alone and had to serve for the remaining months to superannuate but as an uninvolved, careless person, however, appreciating his conditions all people cooperated with him. He had lost all charm of his life and had become totally alone & aloof. Amit had come to attend the last rites but he stayed only for a couple of days and asked his father to come and stay with him but his previous experiences were not very motivating for him to go out of his land. He had got all his dreams & plans totally shattered & devastated and was in a dilemma regarding his future. The northeast which had given him a new life, a vibrant life, a life full of melody & music and had given a true life parter in form of Meghna who had just disappeared in the thin air and almighty was so heartless, so merciless, so cruel, so inconsiderate that He did not give him even a moment to have the last glimpse of, the last touch of, the last word with his departing soul mate.

"What an injustice from the supreme being; what sin have I done, that I am being punished at the dusk of my life when the

light is wanted most?" Was continuously haunting him.

Sometimes he felt as if he had entered the limitless black hole of the universe.

The day time during working days were somehow passing by but the Saturdays & Sundays and the whole nights had become Himalayan peaks of pains. He was totally run down and had lost sense of living and being a human. People had all sympathy for him, they had tried their best to take him out of jungle of agony & pains but nothing worked and month after month passed by.

Month of December was over, new year had commenced and the bell had started moving to ring the last. He could see that after a couple of months all those who were coming to him would disappear and he would be all alone and then how to counter that loneliness was the million-dollar question to him. He knew that he could not live without Meghna and also he would never like to get her memories vanished. One day he received a phone call from his child hood friend Ramesh who was enquiring about him; and listening to his dilemma regarding his life ahead, he suggested him to come back to his old place and reside in his father's house which had been rented out. The company of old friends would be more soothing than being at a far off place alone. That idea somehow struck to Mridul.

"Will you help me to re-establish again at my old place? Who else amongst my old friends and well wishes are still there?" He *enquired from Ramesh.*

"Your best well-wisher Mani and many of us are there, better you come here."

"Let me see."

He had moved out of his place of origin and had come far off to forget Malini and now he had to return back to same square one to escape haunting memories of Meghna but he never liked good name of Meghna to die. He had left his office work to his second in command and was fully concentrating on his future arrangements. He met the people of the service organization with which Meghna was associated and at length decided to make a Meghna Welfare Trust. He struck a deal to sell out his bungalow and most of his assets except those of Meghna and completed all formalities of forming the trust headed by him which would be totally devoted to alleviate the sufferings of underprivileged people and for empowerment of women folk in the north-east region.

1st of April; he became a free, independent, unbounded but useless individual with only one mission to see that Meghna Welfare Trust started functioning and completing winding up to move away. First week of May he had landed back in the same house which he had left over thirty-five years back in search of freedom from the haunting memories of Malini. And see the act of destiny that now he had come back to be away from the fragrance of having become invisible Meghna yet keeping her memories alive.

"What an irony of fate; what a jugglery of God; what benefit is He getting of troubling me?"

He went on pondering over and over but could not get any clue as to what all had happened and why had he come back to the place which had become something unknown for over decades.

By & by he got settled but without any vision, without any mission, without any energy without any life, nothing to look ahead, nothing to gain and having nothing to lose any more but with mountains of memories on his head. Gradually he began mixing with his child hood and school days' friends but found them having their own lives, their own problems and their own limitations. No doubt he had left the sky but had fallen on the palm tree top and had to seek some avenue as the repose of his remaining life; but despite his best efforts for over several months nothing was in sight which was pinching him very deep and keeping him stirred up from inside and under those situations he was planning to relinquish the normal life and join some other service organization to keep himself occupied.

Over six months had elapsed in such a situation that one day he received a ring which disturbed him extremely like spraying powdered salt over the lacerating burn injuries. He was totally unnerved but gradually he regained and reciprocated to the call. That was the call of his love lost nearly forty years ago and which had gone even out of his imagination. He met her for a brief period and that meeting was most ridiculous. After a few days he again received a ring from the same number and his response as earlier was lukewarm and after a few jiggling he met Malini again and that time she was very apologetic regarding her behavior during the earlier meeting and he was also little mellowed down.

During the next meeting he was little open and frankly asked Malini, why was she alone there and to what she narrated a very detailed & pathetic tale,

"When my father came to know of my intention to marry you, he immediately poured all his anger on my mother and totally cut off my movements outside the house and contacts with my friends and hurriedly arranged my marriage with a professor of the same caste who was a widower and ten years elder to me and had a son & a daughter from his previous wife. I was totally against this marriage but he forced my mother to get that done inviting only very close relatives and friends and being helplessly alone I could not communicate that to any one of my friends. I had fifteen years of just going on life and bore a son. The son & daughter from his previous wife never liked me and their

wrath my son also had to bear. Those two children completed their studies and went abroad maintaining contacts only with father. My son was still studying that my husband who had never told me of his ailments, fell sick and was diagnosed to be suffering from cancer. That was a very difficult period for me. His college people helped and gave me a teaching assignment and while doing teaching I did bachelor of education to become a qualified teacher. After two years of fight against cancer he succumbed leaving entire responsibility of my son on me. My son completed his engineering and joined a reputed private firm where he is still serving and sometimes comes to meet me. I had a liking for this place and purchased a house and shifted here. One day an old acquaintance mentioned about you and from somewhere he collected your contact details and gave that to me"

Malini's life story had melted all the thick ice of misunderstanding, whatever he had nurtured against her all these years but Meghna was his unforgettable elixir of life. The growing friendship between him and Malini were noticed by his friends who advised him to marry her and be together. Malini had also some such thought within herself as living alone was quite a difficult proposition and somewhere guilt of betraying Mridul had always been there with her. One day, She reminding of old days liked to know his opinion about marrying her, not for any carnal desires but just for company and togetherness to which he wanted a clarification from her,

"Now Meghna is my soul mate, though late but she is always with me; will you be able to accept me with her?"

"I understand you are passing through the same stage which would have been there when I had gone out of your life and therefore keeping good things of our past we may christen our present."

"Let me think over again, but what would our children feel?"

"They are mature enough to understand."

"Ok. But still let us give some more time and rethink."

Thereafter they did not talk further on that issue but the loneliness which had engulfed them causing raven darkness forced Mridul to think & rethink and at length he decided to give a worldly shape to their deep buried relations once again.

Seldom the land of origin calls back for the same reason one had left it.

ABOUT THE BOOK

This is the saga of a young researcher, brought up by his widowed mother amidst struggles & strives, who had fallen in love with his long time class mate and both had decided to unite in marital bondage but circumstances betrayed them. He left the place of his origin and moved to north-east of India along with his mother. He came in contact with a highly educated young lady, an East-Pakistan refugee having lost all her family members; and developed a liking for her and ultimately married her. They had a wonderful life and a son keeping his mother happy & satisfied. The untimely demise of mother caused a void which she filled with her services to the underprivileged people located in distant villages of North-East.

The melodious life of the couple for over thirty years came to an abrupt end with accidental demise of the lady during her village tour which shattered and devastated the life of the researcher who sold all his property to establish a welfare trust for the cause of the people she had been serving, in the name of his beloved wife. He at length, came back to his place of origin where circumstances took him back to the old classmate to think of a new life once again.

ABOUT THE AUTHOR

Dr O.P.Yadava is a well-known author having over a dozen of books published through CreateSpace. He is a doctorate in chemistry from the University of Allahabad, India. Author had spent his service life with high energy materials in government of India. After being free from the government service, he is devoting his time & energy for the cause of alleviating sufferings and his writings are inspired from such efforts.

He has touched upon several subjects which have been haunting modern India and has always tried to portray struggles & strives which are being encountered by common people who are aspiring to come up in their lives and also of such people who are trying to help them.

****